Automotive Solutions
With SAP

By Ralph Kierberg

bf
Publishing

bookforces publishing
2016

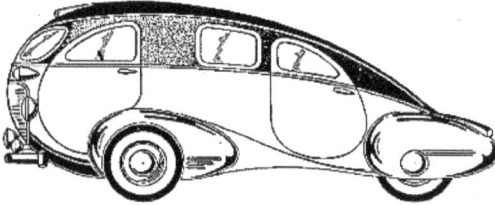

Fig. 1.

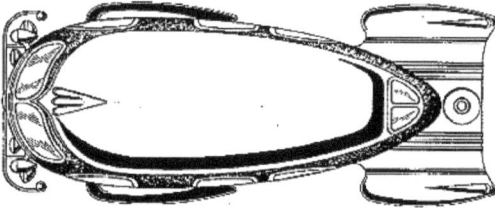

Fig. 2.

Inventor
Clifford Brooks Stevens
By
Attorney

The automotive industry is well known for being one of the most innovative, and with growing, global race for market share, it is a challenge to persistently retaining this edge of innovation and superiority leadership.

The knowhow offered by this book is based on extensive industry knowledge and many years of experiences in the automotive industry.

Automotive Solutions with SAP is the Essential Practice Reference to understand Solutions concepts, designs and how to tailor it to. Receive tips and detailed expert guidance. Maximize your value stream and walk through practical implementation examples.

Automotive Solutions with SAP includes specific topic related examples that are based on years of experience. Gain the knowledge of key concepts and you will be able to make informed decision and lead your automotive project to be more successful.

Automotive Solutions with SAP offers insides to differentiat through vehicle innovation, to reduce operational costs, react quickly on market changes, and increasing productivity. Automotive companies must innovate quicker, increase efficiency, and manufacture more vehicles based on specific customer requirements.

This book explains how to tailor SAP to your fit your specific automotive challenges within production, variant configuration modeling, supply-to-line, use 40 characters as material number, backflush, model planning, sequencing, as well as integration the supply chain process.

bf
Publishing

www.bookforces.com

Published by bookforces publishing – Miami USA

First published and printed in the United States of America.

10 9 8 7 6 5 4 3 2 1

Copyright © 2016 by Ralph Kierberg

Revision 2

First Edition: October 2015

The Library of Congress has cataloged the hardcover edition as follows:

Kierberg, Ralph
    Automotive Solutions with SAP / by Ralph Kierberg – 2nd
    ed.
    p.cm.

ISBN 978-0-9969985-0-5

Dedication

I have two great loves, my family and SAP. To my lovely wife LouLou, my children Sabrina and Sami, and to those who inspired me.

To caffeine and sugar, my companions through many long night of writing

Thank you. Without your support and patience, I would have never achieved my dream.

RALPH KIERBERG

Table of Contents

Acknowledgements

I would like to thank my family; without their help this book would never have been completed. Thank you for your patience and guidance, your use of the editor's red pen and to support me in this long process.

WARNING

I am true of heart!

The whole SAP thing in this book

maybe all wrong.

But if so,

it's all right!

Foreword

This book is based on my experience leading automotive projects. It includes specific topic related examples that are based on this experience and will help you to gain the knowledge of key concepts and designs. The knowledge that you are gaining will support you in making your own key design decision and leading your automotive project to be successful.

One of the main issues is the dramatic shift the automakers make to integrate and interact with dealers, customers, internal control and suppliers. This requires a detailed MRP and supply planning of each part that is required in each vehicle and with that creates a huge data demand. The automotive company need to know when each part (day and time) is required on the production line at what work station, as well as the detailed supply chain planning in the future using Hana presents a huge, new opportunity for automotive companies to meet the increasing demand of more detailed supply to line, quick production planning and scheduling adjustments and plan simulations.

Let say, your automotive factory is producing over 1,000 cars a day, with 20 to 30,000 parts. A detailed, sub-daily production schedule is required for all parts D+15 (today plus 15 days) that is sequenced per day, per shop and per production line, so that production supply can be driven to all the 30 workstations on the production line. A detailed daily supply planning is required for D+15 to M+2. The sub-daily and daily demand calculation of each production supply combined with the demand planning for purchasing integrated to suppliers requires in summary terra bytes of database records. This big data demand is characterized by the tremendous volume and by multiple data sources (SAP tables). To sustain changes in the supply chain or internal on the production floor, the automotive industry is often sacrificing the need for speed (fast results to make decisions) by prioritizing these impacts:

- Rapidly change of the detailed production line sequence due to an unforeseen event
- Capitalize on supply chain opportunities or consolidation production line optimization
- Optimize the global value chain through quick adjustments and simulations

This book will help you achieve your business objectives by applying the solution that is best suited for your key business processes.

Preface

Dear Reader,

Ralph Kierberg is director of advisory with expertise in managing SAP projects and high performing teams. He has led multiple innovative SAP automotive projects. He began his SAP career in 1992, and trust me: He saw lots of SAP products; he was leading customers in Aerospace & Defense, Automotive, Car Engines, and also Industrial Products, Chemicals and Consumer Goods to complete their implementation and business transformation.

An experienced leader with expertise identifying core business requirements and implement a SAP solution to meet specific objectives and operational strategies. A mentor and leader of the SAP Global Network, a platform for SAP professionals worldwide to develop collaborative relationships without borders. The SAP Global Networks connects more than 5,600 professionals to gain benefits from a social business collaboration to solve real business situations and problems.

To be successful in a complex and life-long venture requires love to do the job and in short Ralph brings his dedication and excitement to the client to make the project successful. His network of partners, advisors, mentors and other SAP professional that he uses to find answers and solutions, makes him a person that you want to have around in a project. Success is all about collaboration and sharing, and this is what this book will provide to you.

Be successful

Innovate and deliver a "customer-centric" solution - Accelerate collaborative product innovation - Plan and manufacture efficiently and profitable while plan and react to changes while avoiding disruptions in the production line

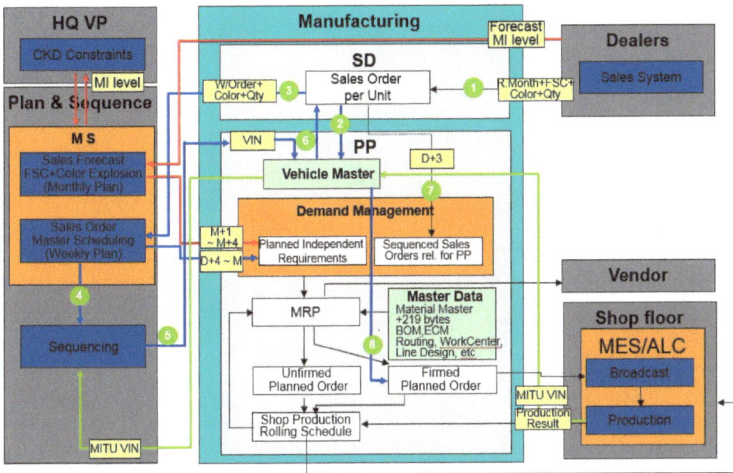

Example of a SAP solution, using multiple functions from long/mid-term planning, sales to sequencing, manufacturing and shop floor MES system integration.

Chapter 1: Automotive Goals & Scope

Businesses in the automotive industry is facing growing pressures to progress on efficiency, reduce costs, and to promptly recognize and respond to a changing market. To increase brand value and increase market share, automotive original equipment manufacturers (OEMs) are faced to produce high-quality vehicles that meet the increasingly sophisticated customers' requirements. The constantly increasing race to compete promotes further the need for innovation and speed. To face these market challenges, the automotive value chain - from OEMs, suppliers, and third parties to dealerships - will benefit from an automotive SAP solution that integrates the specific challenges by focusing on the following:

- Enriched brand management through empathy of market segments and be able to make the vehicle customizable with features that will appeal
- Rapid new product development cycles or adopting changes to accelerate time to market
- Improved manufacturing methods that reduce the time to respond to changes on the fly
- Reduced engineering and production costs through economies of scale in design and production
- Improve logistic execution and supply chain management

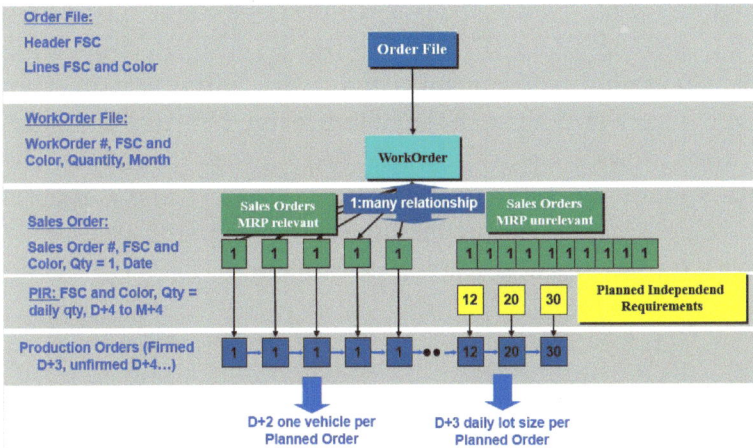

Example: Make-to-Order (MTO) solution that shows the relationship be-

Make-To-Order with Sales Order 1 vehicle

tween the WorkOrder, Sales Order related to production orders and how PIRs (Planned Independent Requirements) are consumed by Sales Orders.

The key is designing and implementing an automotive solution by using the strength of SAP functionality in the automotive industry to deliver these goals and improve businesses. The automotive solution that is explained in this book is designed specific for the automotive industry and support business processes that span organizational boundaries, and integrate key functions including supply chain management, customer relationship management, product life-cycle management, manufacturing, enterprise resource management, and business intelligence. The automotive solution explained is a key element to support these complex processes and is scalable for other OEMs.

The automotive solution documented in this book, allows you to benefit from this scalable, flexible solution that can expand and adapt as requirements change over time.

Today, many automotive companies have chosen SAP as the main solution provider, however many have not implemented a full scale solution for production, because of the huge challenges within production and the required details to run a sufficient production line. Many automotive companies today are still using custom, homemade legacy systems that they have learned to trust and manage or used some sort of hybrid SAP/Legacy solution. The automotive solution documented in this book, is live and is used in multiple vehicle manufacturing facilities fully integrated into supply to line with JIT, supply in sequence, or Kanban.

1.1 Scope of the Automotive Solution

This describe scope and objective to provide a solution with enhanced production control. In this defined Automotive Solution, we have approached the planning with and without APO. These are the main scope definitions that are mastered:

- Operate three shift operations at all manufacturing locations
- Ability to produce multiple models
- Operate multiple plants
- Support Customer Specific Build to Order requirements
- Support Global Standardization
- Material Management
- Purchasing
- Inventory Management including bar code reading and RF/Auto ID (processing)
- Physical Inventory - cycle counting
- Invoice Verification
- BI in combination with Purchasing Information System & Logistics Information System
- Logistics Execution - Inbound & Outbound processes
- Production Planning
- Repetitive Manufacturing
- Parts Distribution Center planning and supply
- Variant Configuration with Classification
- Controlling (product costing)

- Sales & Distribution including interface to external sales systems
- Industry Solution Adoption Automotive
- Planning, Tracking, and Executing Inbound Deliveries (container tracking)
- Production Backflush
- Scheduling Agreement
- EDI Scenarios for Automotive
- Supplier integration - Supplier Workplace
- APO or using ECC as a solution with special focus on sub-daily requiremenst
- Demand Planning
- Supply Chain Cockpit
- Alert Monitor
- Supply Network Planning
- Production Planning and Detailed Scheduling
- Takt times
- Outbound logistics
- Vehicle Identification Numbers
- Sequencing

While the above main scope areas do not show end-to-end processes or an all-inclusive list of sub-processes, the breakdown into the major process areas fit together logically to form a complete scope.

Chapter 2: Manufacturing and Procurement

With support for all automotive manufacturing strategies, a complete SAP solution helps automotive companies to manage the full range of manufacturing activities, from planning to execution and analysis, in a single, end-to-end system. The SAP solution delivers all elements of a customer-oriented manufacturing management system. By combining information from a variety of business processes (including planning, cost accounting, human resources management, materials management, warehouse management, plant maintenance, and quality management), the SAP solution supports the development and execution of efficient production plans and ensures that accurate, comprehensive information is available at any time.

By using this SAP solution effectively in conjunction with the Just-in-Time Process for Suppliers application, businesses in the automotive industry can leverage just-in-time processes to improve responsiveness and reduce the complexity of obtaining automotive components and subcomponents. The solution supports inbound calls based on sales and forecasted orders as well as outbound calls for replenishment based on Kanban methodology. As a result, the automotive company can develop effective supply chain processes that address changing demands throughout the value chain, improve efficiencies, and reduce manufacturing time and costs.

			Production			

Master data	Vehicle Planning & scheduling	Vehicle Production Execution	Vehicle production control	MIP Planning & Scheduling	MIP production Execution	MIP production control
• Material master • Production version • Configurable BOM • Sales order BOM • MIP BOM • AS BOM • Routing • Work center • Work calendar • Shift schedule • Line design • Tack time (UPH) • Reporting point • HPCS code • ECM • Legacy BOM interface	• Work order management • ALC code mgt • VIN master management • Master production planning • Sequencing vehicle order • Body input schedule • Trim input schedule • VIN Spec change • Daily MRP • MRP list • Sub-daily MRP • APS interface	• Reporting point backflush • Final backflush • Backflush error mgt • MES interface	• Sequence parts schedule • Production status report • Production status by shop • WIP status by shop • Production status by work order • Spec change status • Production trouble management • Productivity KPI management (Utilization, troubled cars stayed in shop etc)	• Master production planning • Production plan list • Daily MRP • MRP list	• Pull list • Final backflush • Backflush error mgt • MES interface	• Production status report • Production status by shop • Production trouble management • Productivity KPI management (Utilization etc)

SAP standard screen
&
Custom development Screen

Supply to line	MRP	Backflush
• Pull list • WM • PSA	• Daily MRP run • Long term MRP • MRP list	• Hourly • 2stepReporting point • Results and Error Log • Final Backflush

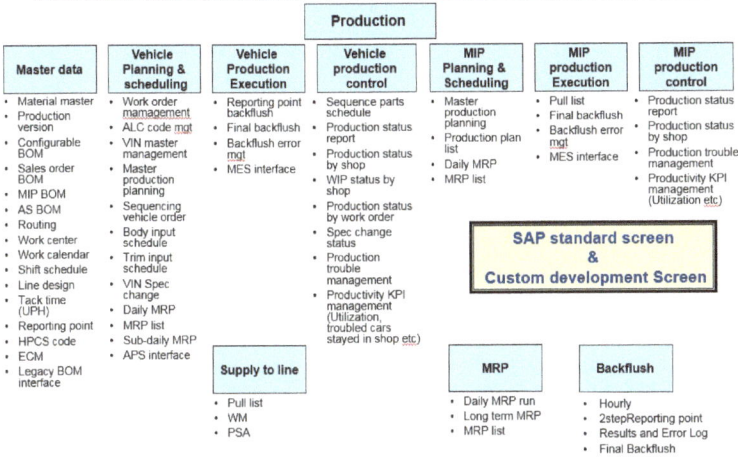

Example: Scope of the SAP Production Solution

2.1 Backflush

The challenge within the automotive industry is that within a specific tact time, let say a minute, a car is produced and the regular backflush is not fast enough. Not fast enough to update the inventory, post the financials and costing for all the thousands of parts required to backflush. In other words, the first backflush is still busy posting in the background and the next backflush is already executed. Not having the backflush completed, will impact your inventory accuracy on the production line and will eventually interrupt the flow of raw materials required to run the production line (supply to line).

But first things first, normal SAP back flushing is the automatic goods issue, financial and costing posting and the consumption out of the PSA (Production Supply Area or Work Center on the line) via WM. SAP will automatically posts the goods issue when you confirm the operations. Backflush provides the option to perform Goods Issuance automatically, as soon as the Auto-ID or RFID passes a PSA the production records confirms that the production line step has been produced. When this happens, back flushing is triggered to automatically update and record the quantity of the materials used in producing the production order (vehicle with VIN number) as well as their associated financial values under the Cost of Goods Manufactured (COGM).

Example: How back flush on the production line interacts with the PSA (Production Supply Area) stock level. The PSA raw mate-

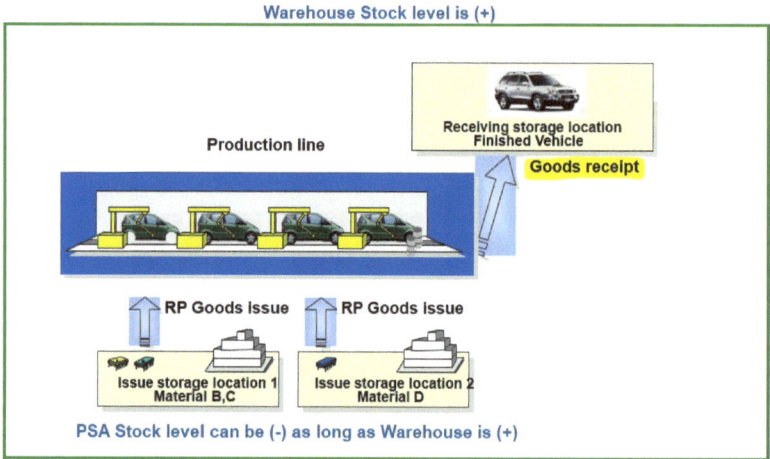

rial is resupplied by each shift by using the detailed production schedule to cMESulate where on what work-center (PSA) material is required for the next x hours.

At the end of the line, the automatic goods receipts function will be triggered to perform Goods Receipt automatically on recording confirmation.

The automatic backflush initiates multiple sub-transactions and should only be used for real time postings if the throughput of the database is faster as the time between backflushes. If there is not enough time to finish the background postings or when planning products with many variants and large numbers of orders is required, as in the automotive industry, a much faster process is required.

2.2 Rapid Backflush

The rapid backflush is IPPE based and APO can be used, however in this example APO was determine to be too expensive, so the APO rapid backflush was installed within standard SAP ECC.

The production is Make-to-Order (MTO), the planned orders for the vehicle with an individual VIN number are for the product ordered by the customer (dealer) and important components are assigned to the pegged customer order.

Example: Line Hierarchy with multiple shops and different re-

Line Hierarchy

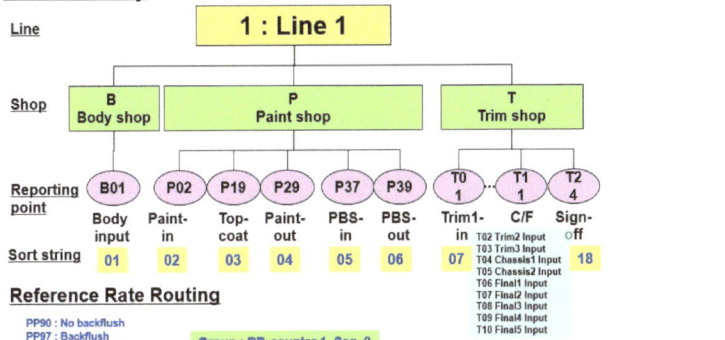

Line		**1 : Line 1**

| Shop | **B** Body shop | **P** Paint shop | **T** Trim shop |

Reporting point	**B01**	**P02**	**P19**	**P29**	**P37**	**P39**	**T0 1**	...	**T1 1**	**T2 4**
	Body input	Paint-in	Top-coat	Paint-out	PBS-in	PBS-out	Trim1-in		C/F	Sign-off
Sort string	01	02	03	04	05	06	07			18

T02 Trim2 Input
T03 Trim3 Input
T04 Chassis1 Input
T05 Chassis2 Input
T06 Final1 Input
T07 Final2 Input
T08 Final3 Input
T09 Final4 Input
T10 Final5 Input

Reference Rate Routing

PP90 : No backflush
PP97 : Backflush
PP99 : Backflush & GR

Group : RP, counter 1, Seq. 0

OP	0010	0020	0030	0040	0050	0060	0070	0080	0090	0100	0110	0120	0130	0140	0150	0160	0170	0180
CB Key	PP97	PP97	PP90	PP90	PP90	PP97	PP90	PP97	PP97	PP97	PP97	PP97	PP97	PP97	PP97	PP97	PP97	PP99
RP	B01	P02	P19	P29	P37	P39	T01	T02	T03	T04	T05	T06	T07	T08	T09	T10	T11	T24
Sort string (BP)	01	02	(03)	(04)	(05)	06	(07)	08	09	10	11	12	13	14	15	16	17	18

porting points, where some operations trigger a backflush.

The PSA (Production Supply Area) is used in our example to use production schedule and warehouse operations to supply raw material into the production line. The production supply is initiated per shift, wave planning, and for some directly into the line. The PSA is an area within the production line or shop where products or raw materials are staged for later withdrawal via backflush. To stage products for the production line consolidation multiple a production order from the detailed scheduling, the SAP WM module must know where it has to take the products or raw materials. For each production orders in SAP the PSA contains this information. For WM (or

EWM) the PSA is usually a storage bin where the raw material can be staged.

In other words, the Production supply areas (PSAs) are used for material replenishment and are situated directly on the shop floor. The supply area groups work centers near production storage bins based on the material staging methods.

The reporting point backflush combined with the PSA can be used to withdraw components closer to the real-time where they are required within the operation, as well as the WIP (Work in Process) can be cMESulated and if required a detailed scrap quantity can be backflushed to a specific operation.

For smaller production volumes the end-reporting can be used to backflush all parts consumed as well as to report the goods receipt of the vehicle.

See the next example of reporting points, backflush points and PSA to evaluate the relationships between them.

Example: How PSA, reporting points and backflush points are related.

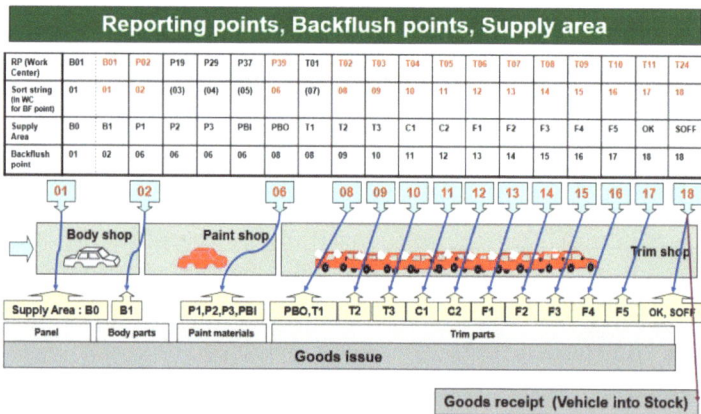

Reporting points, Backflush points, Supply area

RP (Work Center)	B01	B01	P02	P19	P29	P37	P39	T01	T02	T03	T04	T05	T06	T07	T08	T09	T10	T11	T24
Sort string (in WC for BF point)	01	01	02	(03)	(04)	(05)	06	(07)	08	09	10	11	12	13	14	15	16	17	18
Supply Area	B0	B1	P1	P2	P3	PBI	PBO	11	12	T3	C1	C2	F1	F2	F3	F4	F5	OK	SOFF
Backflush point	01	02	06	06	06	06	08	08	09	10	11	12	13	14	15	16	17	18	18

01   02   06   08   09   10   11   12   13   14   15   16   17   18

Body shop   Paint shop   Trim shop

Supply Area : B0	B1	P1,P2,P3,PBI	PBO,T1	T2	T3	C1	C2	F1	F2	F3	F4	F5	OK, SOFF
Panel	Body parts	Paint materials						Trim parts					

Goods issue

Goods receipt (Vehicle into Stock)

If you use reporting point backflushing, the system backflushes all material components that have been consumed and posts the activities carried out at the reporting point operation. It reduces the dependent requirements in the planned orders and updates the statistics in the LIS. For the rapid backflush, only the inventory posting is executed at the time of backflush and the financial and costing posting is initiated at the end of the shift or end of the day. These safes a lot of horse-power and makes the backflush much faster, so that the rapid backflush can be used for real-time backflush.

In our example we are using the mandatory reporting point backflush, to be able to backflush scrap directly at the operation. If you use mandatory reporting point backflushing, you post the quantity that is on the production line at that point in time, for each reporting point. You receive a material posting document for each reporting point. Mandatory reporting point backflush guarantees maximum control over the operation, however. When you carry out the WIP posting you are using the mandatory reporting point backflush processing to cMESulate required reporting.

Example: Integration of Manufacturing Broadcast with Production Confirmation

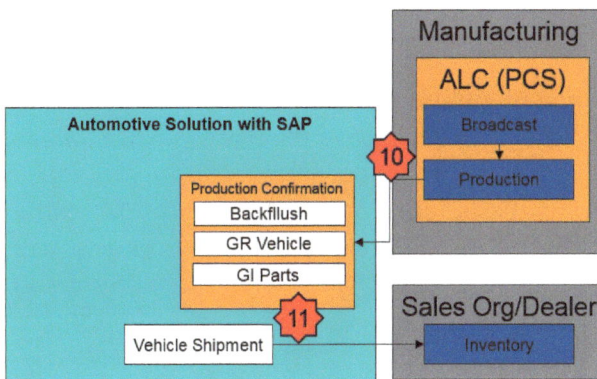

The MES (PCS) system is collecting vehicle reporting point information's per VIN # either via production confirmation on the line or via Auto-ID passing the reporting point. The transferred data initiates the SAP back flush per reporting point and planned order as well as the production completion for a vehicle (end of line). After the finishing of a vehicle the vehicle will be shipped out of inventory as soon as it passes the money gate (parking lot). SAP sent shipping information to the sales organization to organize the transportation to the correct dealer.

2.3 Long Term Planning

For our automotive solution, a Long Term Planning (LTA) was used, this was based on the decision to reduce cost and to not use APO. In order to provide support for long-term production planning and for carrying out simulations in short and mid-term planning multiple scenarios are used to carry out an annual planning or a rolling quarterly planning run you require information on the future stock and requirements situation. This requires that the planner need to know how sales and operations planning (SOP) will influence resources. That is, whether the results of sales planning can actually be produced with capacity on hand. If such information is available it is possible to decide at an early date whether extra capacity (increase temporary workforce, overtime or weekend work) will be required to cope with bottlenecks, or whether sub-assembly may be purchased from the main production facility instead of produced at the plant.

In long-term planning you can also plan materials that usually require very little planning in operative planning, such as, materials planned using reorder point planning, bulk material, and materials planned using KANBAN. In long-term planning, you can plan these materials as you would MRP materials. This provides you with an overview of how these materials influence the demand program.

The purchasing department used their own LTP to have a more detailed result based planning. They use the information on the future requirements quantities to estimate future orders. This provides them with a basis for negotiating delivery schedules and contracts with subcontractors and vendors. Vendors also gain from long-term planning as they are sent a preview of future purchase orders.

Example: Long Term Planning (LTP) for purchasing and annual planning

Purchasing LTP & Annual Planning LTP are Different

	Purchasing LTP	**Annual Planning LTP**
BOM	Selected From Demand Management Production Version (Work Order Spec Version)	Selected From LTP Scenario Usage : 6 (Costing)
Routing	Selected From Demand Management Production Version (Work Order Spec Version)	Selected From IMG Configuration Usage : 10 (Costing)
LTP Scenario & DM Version	We will use '999' Scenario We will use '99' DM Version	We will use '0XX' Scenario for 20XX Year We will use 'XX' DM Version for 20XX Year

For annual planning, scenarios and DM versions should be defined to cover each year, for example year 2018 scenario 018, year 2019 scenario 019, and DM 18 and 19.

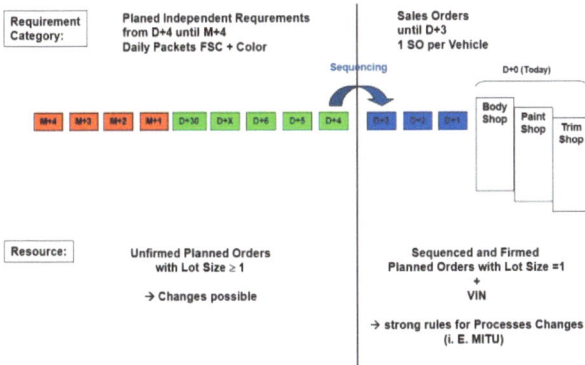

Example: Daily requirements four month in the future, sequencing the vehicles through the different shops is three days in the future.

2.4 Master Data for Vehicle Production

Off course there are the usual BoM (Bill of Material), remember in our example we did not use APO and IPPE, and there are work centers and routings and documents (DMS), however we also needed a Vehicle Master. A vehicle master is normally defined via VMS (Vehicle Management System), however based on cost rea-

Category	Routing for vehicle scheduling		Routing for vehicle costing
	Line design	Reference rate routing	Rate routing
Scheduling	Basis of vehicle scheduling	Basis of vehicle scheduling	No use
Capacity	Available capa. · Work calendar · Periodic working hours per shift	None	None
Costing	No use	No use	Labor costing for FSC · Standard cost estimate · Product cost collector
Backflush	No use	Backflush point for component backflush	Actual labor cost backflush - Issue : relationship with backflush points
Work center	Line, Shop, Reporting point	Reporting point	Work centers for Cost centers
Elements	Material & no of takts	Sequence of RPs	Summarized man hours and machine hours per work center for each FSC
Level	Plant (1 set)	Plant (1 set)	FSC (as many as FSC)
Owner	Production control	Production control	Engineering & Production

sons, VMS was not used and therefore the equipment master was used as vehicle master. The vehicle master stored the VIN number, as well as other key components like the engine (engine master was "married" with vehicle master) as well as production specs including the result of the sequence planning run to provide exact production times of when this VIN will pass what work center. The planned production time per work center could be compared with the actual production history, for research and reporting purpose.

In our SAP system, the equipment master used as base configuration the 'fleet object' was copied into the vehicle master. In addition to the normal components of the equipment master record, the following vehicle relevant data is available in the SAP solution:

- Identification data (for example, VIN number, chassis number)
- Measurement data (for example, height, width)
- Transport-relevant data (for example, weight, maximum load weight, maximum load volume)

- Further attributes (for example, interior color, exterior color, key number)
- Engine data (for example, engine type, engine power, cubic capacity)
- And classification vehicle defined screen section for relevant data

In addition, the vehicle master allowed to track warranty related claims and spare parts (exact key replacement).

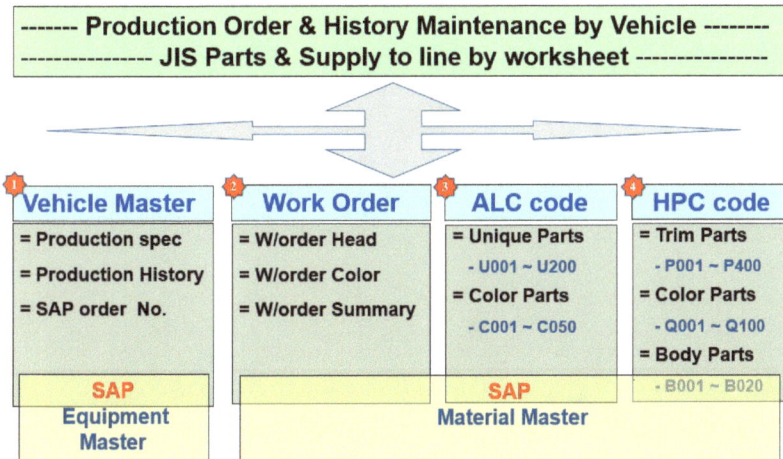

------- **Production Order & History Maintenance by Vehicle** --------
--------------- **JIS Parts & Supply to line by worksheet** ----------------

Vehicle Master	**Work Order**	**ALC code**	**HPC code**
= Production spec	= W/order Head	= Unique Parts	= Trim Parts
= Production History	= W/order Color	- U001 ~ U200	- P001 ~ P400
= SAP order No.	= W/order Summary	= Color Parts	= Color Parts
		- C001 ~ C050	- Q001 ~ Q100
			= Body Parts
SAP		**SAP**	- B001 ~ B020
Equipment Master	**Material Master**		

Example: Vehicle Master, Work Order, MES code and HPC code (code used to display a part on a shop floor screen)

The material master was used to define a specific work order. The MES code was used to ensure that a new configuration of a vehicle was logically correct. The HPC code was used in the production to identify visually using characters and colors to identify a part/component that need to be installed into the vehicle. (More details later).

Example: Vehicle Master with all data blocks

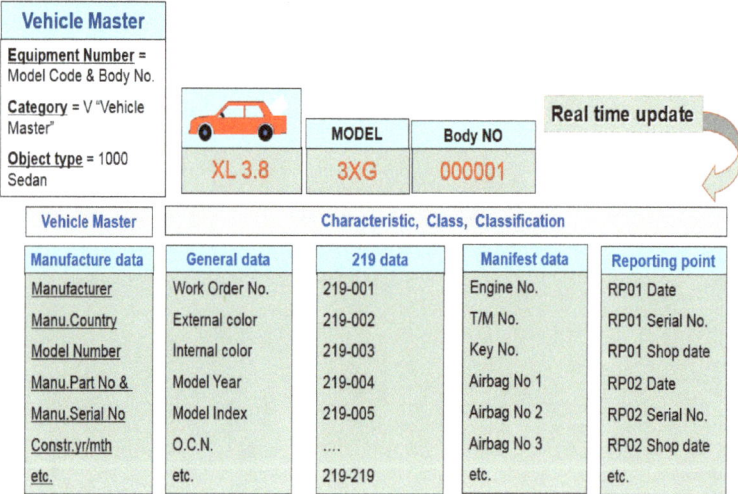

The vehicle master is the vehicle specific data that collects all relevant information about the vehicle, serial number, VIN, body

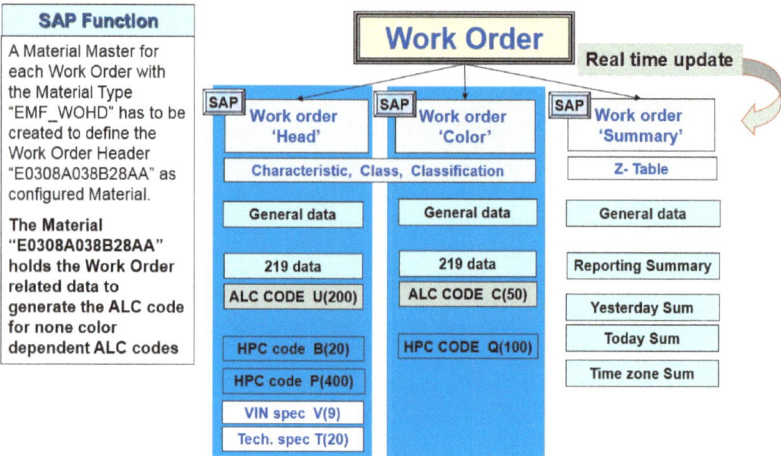

number and other information required for production, sales and after-market.

Example: Work Order data used for MES and production

We are using VC (Variant Configuration) for our example automotive solution with SAP. VC is used for the sales cycle (dealer portal) as well as to find available inventory at a dealer location and/or to find available inventory as partial match to the customer wish list, for example there is a black car available with leather fully loaded.

The work order is used to capture/define the configured vehicle, what can be received into inventory, from the configurable vehicle, cannot be stored in available inventory.

2.5 Engine Production based on Vehicle Production

Off course there are the usual BoM (Bill of Material), remember in our example we did not use APO and IPPE, and You sell a large number of engines per year and you need to produce for the vehicle manufacturing. You control the production of the engines by annual planning. Incoming sales orders as well as vehicle demands are subtracted from the planning and planned requirements are replaced by actual requirements. The engines are made-to-stock and when a customer/dealer places an order, an engine is taken from stock and delivered.

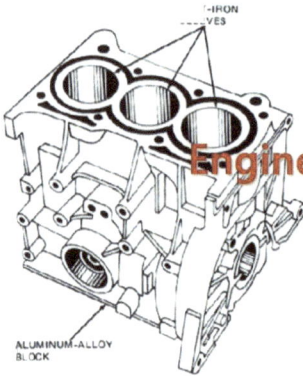

Fig. 13-1 Cylinder block for an inline three cylinder engine.
(*Chevrolet Division of General Motors Corporation*)

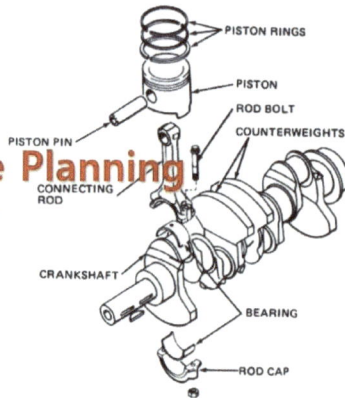

Fig. 11-8 Crankshaft with one piston-and-connecting-rod

A specialty of the vehicle manufacturing is that the right engine need to be "married" with the right vehicle. In other words, the engines need to be sequenced based on the detailed vehicle production schedule.

2.6 Sub-Daily Requirements for Supply to Line

An automotive SAP solution requires sub-daily requirements with a time stamp with hours, minutes and seconds to control the vehicle production line. If you are using APO and IPPE, that is exactly what you get, but is there an alternative without using APO?

In this book is was often mentioned that the automotive client and that is the SAP solution explained in this book, wanted to reduce production cost as well as implementation cost. APO was ruled out to be too expensive and standard ECC was used. In this SAP solution the RESB table was extended to add the sequence number and time stamp to it. This was a custom solution that integrated with vehicle sequencing to have a accurate picture of the demand specific to the vehicle. This allowed for a sub-daily schedule of parts that are delivered into the line via external vendor (example seats) or internal production schedule (example engine).

Chapter 3: Variant Configuration Modeling

In the automotive industry, the number of potential variations that can be specified in customer orders presents particular challenges throughout the entire supply chain. To help better manage this customization, SAP VC (Variant Configuration) is used to integrate configuration capabilities that help sales and planners closely align the model mix with market demands. Variant Configuration (VC) is fully integrated with planning, pricing, order processing, availability checking, production, fulfillment, billing, and financial reporting, and ensures a consistent view of the product in sales orders, production plans, and profitability analyses.

Example: Variant Configuration Process

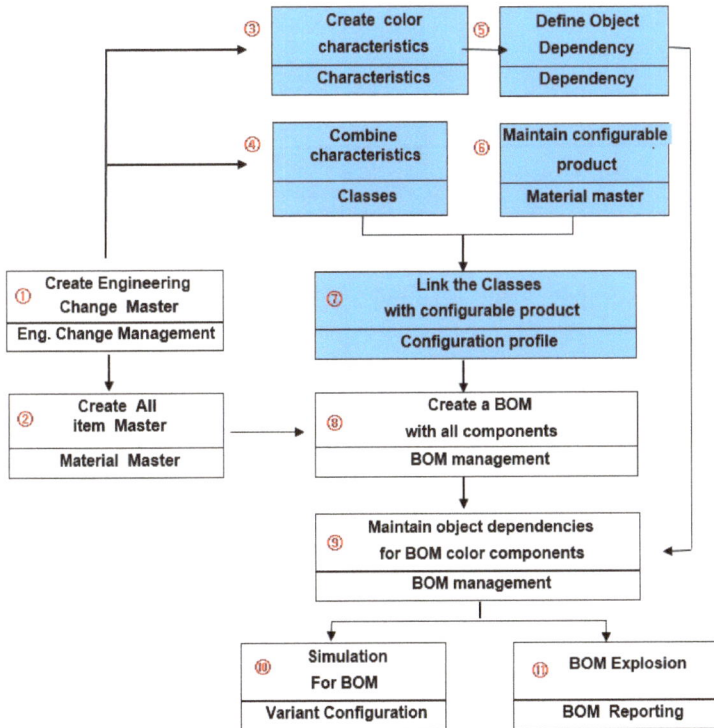

③	Create color characteristics	⑤	Define Object Dependency
	Characteristics		Dependency

④	Combine characteristics	⑥	Maintain configurable product
	Classes		Material master

①	Create Engineering Change Master
	Eng. Change Management

⑦	Link the Classes with configurable product
	Configuration profile

②	Create All item Master
	Material Master

⑧	Create a BOM with all components
	BOM management

⑨	Maintain object dependencies for BOM color components
	BOM management

⑩	Simulation For BOM
	Variant Configuration

⑪	BOM Explosion
	BOM Reporting

VC is used mainly for three purposes Planning, Product Variant Structure and Search. VC Characteristics and associated values are assigned to the product master in order to classify them. This allows the users to locate the required data without the knowledge of the part master number, based on properties of the part that is subject to search. The SuperBOM structure and variant definitions are created with classification and related functions such as dependencies. Characteristics based planning is used as an environment to execute forecasts not only for product families, but also for geographical regions. For vehicles a VC solution is utilized to manage

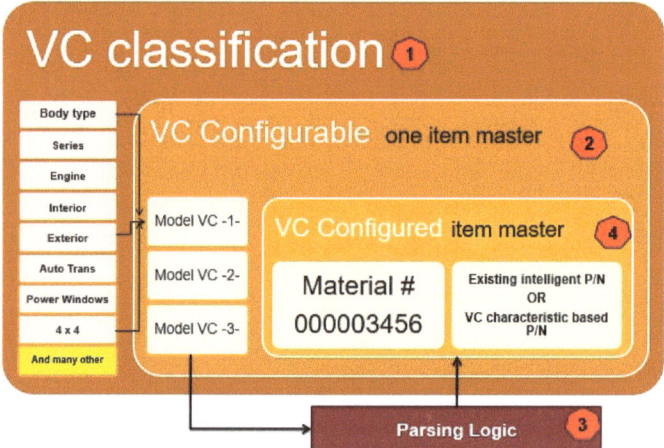

integrated BOM and routing, to support the highly integrated process of product development for multi-variant products. For Engines and parts kit assembly, simple BOM and Routing structure are used.

3.1 Full Spec Code Identifies the Configuration

Each vehicle variant is identified by the Full Spec Code (FSC) number. This number basically represents the configuration of the sales order/vehicle and is divided into sections. The FSC is a material number which identifies the configuration of the vehicle and uses an intelligent number range.

▶ Configuration Example

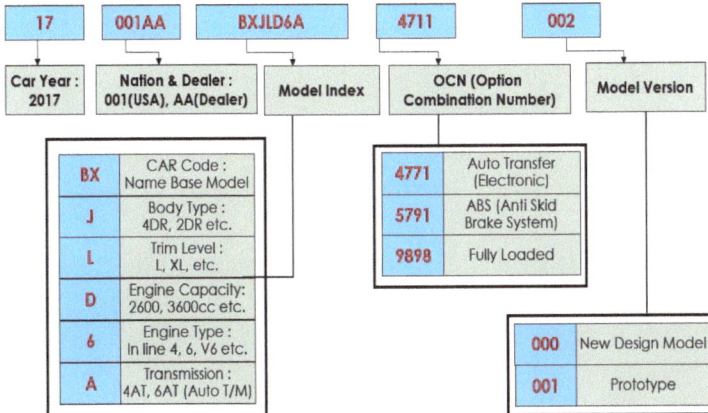

17	001AA	BXJLD6A	4711	002

Car Year: 2017	Nation & Dealer: 001(USA), AA(Dealer)	Model Index	OCN (Option Combination Number)	Model Version

BX	CAR Code : Name Base Model
J	Body Type : 4DR, 2DR etc.
L	Trim Level : L, XL, etc.
D	Engine Capacity: 2600, 3600cc etc.
6	Engine Type : In line 4, 6, V6 etc.
A	Transmission : 4AT, 6AT (Auto T/M)

4771	Auto Transfer (Electronic)
5791	ABS (Anti Skid Brake System)
9898	Fully Loaded

000	New Design Model
001	Prototype

A demand on the FSC number is the result of the vehicle forecast and sales order process in the SAP VC environment. This demand is passed on in form of a planned independent requirement using a finished goods material.

- Enable the forecast of vehicles
- Enable the creation of independent requirements by FSC number
- Enable the production of vehicles based on the FSC number
- Enable the costing of the vehicle
- The FSC code is 17 characters and is the material number in SAP, however if more than 18 characters are required, the material master short description can be used to store the FSC number
- The version is represented in the production version of the material master
- The interior color and exterior color is a characteristic added to the VC

Chapter 4: Core Logistic

This chapter describes all the key elements and business processes required in SAP for the vehicle planning and execution process. It represents a closed, integrated and consistent process chain of elements required to manufacture vehicles. This chapter has been subdivided into three main process streams and represents the 'core process vehicle'.

- 'Sales' is the process stream focusing on customer facing side of the supply chain and consists of Vehicle Sales and Parts Sales.
- 'Production Planning' is the process stream focusing on the optimization of the manufacturing process and consists of Demand Planning, Monthly Planning, Weekly Planning, and Daily Planning.
- 'Vehicle Assembly' is designed as a closed cycle of elements required for the manufacturing of vehicles. These elements consist of Vehicle Manufacturing, Production Backflush, MES, etc.
- 'Engine Assembly' describes the third process from Sequencing of the Engine Orders, Production Control, Engine Work Orders, and Production backflush.
- Other underlying scope elements that are addressed in this section are Material (Parts) Planning, Inventory Management, Master Data, Data Conversion, and Interfaces.

4.1 Sales / Vehicle Parts Ordering

The vehicle ordering process initiates the production execution process and Transformed into the SAP environment, firm Dealer orders covering a limited short-term horizon are pulled in to order file. Firm Dealer orders are represented in SAP by Sales Orders including vehicle specific information. Since one Sales order will exist for every vehicle built, unique identifiable information such as the VIN is applied to the Sales Order upon Serialization. The requirements date of a vehicle being ordered from the Sales organization is the vehicle completion date. Hence, data such as the expected 'vehicle off-line' date will be applied to the SAP Sales Order.

The Sales Order in SAP fulfills the task of triggering the logistics process but will also be used for invoicing purposes. Supplementary to the manufacturing of finished products, a service parts process is accommodated to support the Parts Distribution Center. Service parts may be parts to be procured externally or parts to be manufactured in-house such as engines or body parts. The process chain is similar to materials directly related to the production of vehicles, however, the following is considered:

- SAP Procurement elements of service parts are differentiated from normal production parts (unique identification)
- Different Invoicing and Delivery procedure is set up

4.2 Service Parts / After Market Sales

The Service Parts Business is supporting the aftermarket parts business and the service parts. The service parts business is fully integrated into the SAP world and covers the sales, picking and packing and delivery process. Since the sales order process is a central part of the solution we have identified the following sales order business processes:

a. Standard Order
b. Rush Order – You may need to use two types of rush orders, one for parts orders and one for service parts orders with a specific shipping point to accommodate these orders.
c. Delivery Order – this will support requirement type contracts.

d. Bulk Order – this will be used specifically for commercial parts bulk orders.
e. Return Orders–to reduce complexity a SAP standard return should be used.
f. Debit Memo Request
g. Credit Memo Request
h. Free of Charge Delivery

Two basic types of Sales Orders are used by SAP, a standard order (includes from stock) and a Make-to-Order sales order. Both types of orders can be created either by referencing a previous quote for the material or by entering the order without a previous quote. The Make-to-Order sales order is used for Kits (for example the break kit) and an availability check for the requested parts is a part of the sales order process.

Authorized dealers are directly generating orders for spare parts into the SAP system through a Dealer system interface. These orders will normally be generated without reference to an existing quote. However, the system will be able to process orders both with and without reference. The Dealer system interface will translate the input as necessary to generate the order in SAP.

Note of military parts are required: The service parts organization generate orders by either manually entered or through EDI. Both standard and rush orders will be used. Each part number will be identified separately on an individual line on the quotation form. The order confirmation is generated in the form of paper, electronic and/or EDI outputs.

a. Service parts business – delivery process

The delivery process refers to the shipping activities for a sales order. Delivery processing refers to the process of preparing goods for shipment. Creating a delivery document signals the start of the shipping activities for the product and helps to manage all activities efficiently. When a delivery document is created, critical shipping information (i.e.

Ship-to address, materials, and quantities) is copied from the sales order into the delivery document. These processes / activities include:

1) Picking the product - A transfer order will be created through Warehouse Management for a delivery that is due for picking. These can be created singularly or grouped together as required.

2) Packing the product – Many spare parts operations are using extensive packaging functionality through SAP. Different packing requirements are often driven by customer specific requirements.

3) Planning and Monitoring Shipments – at SAP shipments can be planned manually (specifying one order) or collectively (executing deliveries from a delivery due list). Shipments may also be monitored manually (one order) or grouped collectively (based on shipping point, due date or ship-to address)

4) Prepare shipping papers – Packing lists, bills of lading, export declarations, Hazardous material documentation is being prepared dependent on the sales order and material.

5) Posting goods issue – When a goods issue for a delivery is posted, SAP automatically debit the Cost of Goods Sold account and credit the inventory valuation account. Physical inventory counts are also adjusted. Posting goods issue is a key integration point between the SD and MM and FI modules.

Delivery Pick Tickets for all open deliveries can either be created on-line (immediate for rush orders) or automated via batch and will often be printed directly at the Parts Distribution Center.

    b. Dealer system

In order to integrate and collaborate with dealers closer, the external Dealer system is used by commercial dealers to order spare parts. An interface has been created between the external Dealer system and the SAP system. The SAP system accept dealer orders for parts from Dealer system and reserve a "daily inventory" in the SAP system to block available inventory and mark it as available for dealer parts orders only. At the end of the day the unordered inventory will be released and a new "daily inventory" will be calculated.

c. Kit Production

Spare Parts can be ordered in a bundle that is often referred to as a Kit. These Kit's are a selection of certain spare parts and are often reduced in price. Kits can be produced on stock if they are a part of the demand planning or selectively produced as make-to-order based on the existing sales order. The Kit Production prints pick tickets for the parts that are required. The specific box for the kit can be assigned to the specific kit, for example metal box or plastic box and sometimes is even produced in house.

4.3 Sales / Warranty Management

Warranty management is in most organizations a costly time consuming process. Some Warranty Management systems are still paper based and gives organizations very little visibility on the key information required for business decisions. This Automotive Solution with SAP Warranty Management System (WMS) provides a framework and functionality where the claims are managed electronically either by owners or the dealers. WMS enabled to control dealerships and ensure the highest quality of products over the long-term. It not only provided classification for claims but also capability to analyze data and respond in a timelier and effective manner. Based on classification and the vehicle master (equipment master) certain claims can be processed automatically. Claims that require analysis can be forwarded automatically to the right parts of the organization. A claim contains data on related objects, like vehicles or engines or simply OTC (over the counter) parts, the parts that have been replaced or used to repair the vehicle, and operating hours as well as additional expenses or external services.

Main components of the WMS are Claims, Parts Handling, Reporting and Auditing. Although there are other process flows that are configured as a common scenario are electronic receipts of claims from customers or dealers by OEM, processing the claims and respond automatically or manually based on the category, and sending the response back to the dealer or customer.

The sales brand strategy focused on providing a singular view of the customer as the primary driver throughout the supply chain. Dealers and End-Customers for the different brands access the website to configure vehicles to desired specifications, to obtain vehicle availability information, negotiate payment/warranty terms with dealers, and ultimately accept delivery terms. A "pure" build-to-order (BTO) process may be ideal in delivering exact customer requirements with zero inventory of pre-finished goods. However, the limitation of manufacturing processes, supplier requirements, logistics of vehicle movement, cost, and dealer franchise laws preclude or "constrain" implementation of a pure BTO. In view of this environment this automotive solution mapped out a vision for what has been called a "constrained build to order" CBTO model. In such a model, characteristics of make-to-stock and BTO are blended to meet customers' expectations, while minimizing the operational disruption to the supplier, production, and distribution entities.

The following is a list of items that this automotive solution considered critical for the definition of CBTO business requirements. The italicized items were identified as particularly relevant for integration with the automotive solution project.
- Demand planning.
- *Production scheduling and sequencing system changes to support real time operation for all plants*

- Interfaces to logistics systems & processes supported by vehicle processing centers
- OEM, region, dealer, company vehicle, export accounts, and fleet ordering and forecasting processes
- Specific accessory installation program interface
- Interface to dealer management data
- Interface to the consumer web interface
- *Delivery status feedback to customer internet orders*
- Dealer/customer dialogue for price, financing and warranty negotiations
- *Vehicle specification configuration with marketing and pricing information*
- *Availability search engine for vehicles (dealer inventory, produced inventory and schedule of to-be produced inventory)*
- *Interface to logistics tracking systems*
- *Executive reporting system*

4.4 Production Planning / Demand Planning

Production Planning

Planning & Scheduling

Demand Planning
Monthly Planning
Weekly Planning
Daily Planning

Demand planning is the process to create sales volume forecast applied to monthly and weekly planning. Sales forecast level is for example Nation, Model code and options for monthly planning and full specification level for weekly planning.

Global demand is managed in one system for Global resource planning. Demand planning is reviewed and decided concurrently by related departments using statistical method to forecast demand. Forecast accuracy is reviewed periodically.

Production Planning Strategy			
	Vehicle	56	Characteristics Planning
	Press	40	Planning with final assembly
	Engine	40	Planning with final assembly
The Method of Production			
	Vehicle		Repetitive Manufacturing (REM)
	Press		Discrete Manufacturing
	Engine		Repetitive Manufacturing (REM)

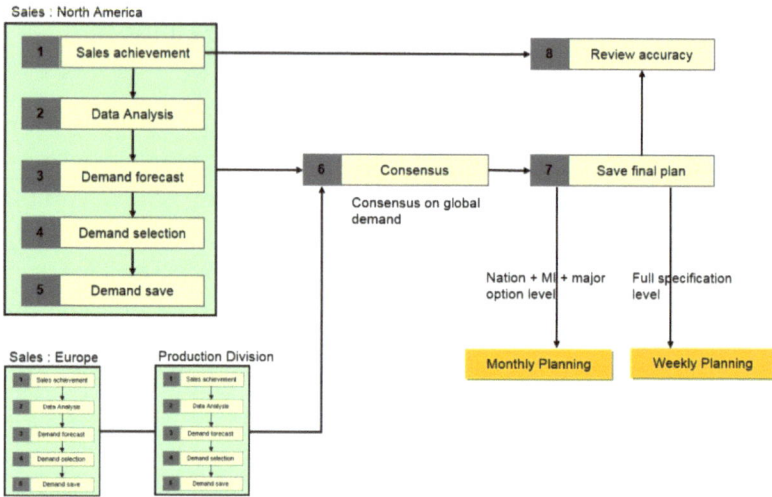

Example: Work Flow Demand Planning

The following demand planning issues are considered:

| 1 | Sales achievement | •Global sales achievements should be gathered periodically. |

•Planner can vary view format changing aggregation level, region, and period.
•Planner can investigate trends using statistical methods.
•Each user can set up his own analysis environment.

2 Data analysis

•Demand forecasting should be executed in planning system and multiple forecasts should be provided using different statistical methods.
•Each user can set up his own forecast function using system.
•Production availability of demand forecasted should be reviewed.

3 Demand forecast

•Multiple forecasts can be viewed in one screen compared with actual achievements.
•User can easily notify best forecast through screen and best forecast can be recommended by system.

4 Demand selection

•Departments related with demand forecast include sales function, finance function, purchasing function, production function, and so on.
•Department to be related with forecast and to have proposal role of forecast should be defined. Each department has it's own forecast scope and responsibility.
•Saved forecast can be viewed by related department concurrently.

5 Demand save

•Related departments concurrently review multiple forecast proposed by each department.
•Rough production capacity will be considered in selecting demand forecast.
•Assumptions, measures, and strategic decisions reflected to forecast selection should be shared.

6 Consensus

•Saved final plan will be imported into the monthly and weekly planning system.

7 Save final plan

•Monthly planning and weekly planning role is how to produce demand considering multiple constraints. What to make is defined in demand planning. So, forecast accuracy should be improved for revenue improvement caused by stock and rushed transportation decrease.
•Periodic accuracy review reveals problems caused by forecast error and make planner to amend the forecast reflecting latest trends.

7 Review accuracy

Production Planning

Planning & Scheduling

Demand Planning
Monthly Planning
Weekly Planning
Daily Planning

Monthly planning is the process to plan each plant's monthly vehicle production and KD parts' delivery plan used in oversea plants. Major option parts' requirement are calculated based on Monthly vehicle production plan. Monthly plan's scope is considering the Plant as well as Global demand and resources and establish global optimized plan. Monthly plan considers available global resources for certain region demand when certain region capacity cannot produce the demand. Oversea plants' KD delivery plan is decided through monthly plan.

Production Planning

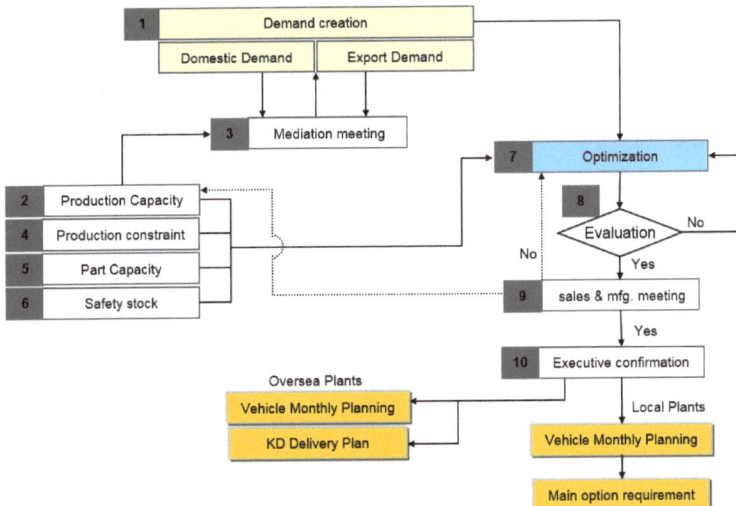

Weekly planning is the process to plan daily vehicle production, MIP parts' requirement, and mid/short term delivery parts' requirement reflecting latest demand status and detail constraints based on monthly planning. Weekly plan should provide foundation to reduce vehicle stock and OTD by reflecting latest customer requirement and multiple constraints to planning. Revenue Increase, flexibility to market change, OTD reduction, Visibility of plan, production competition should be supported by weekly planning.

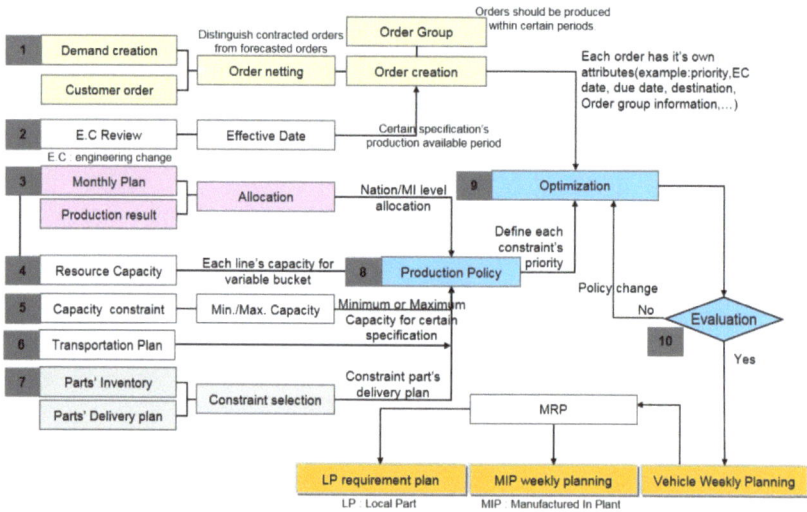

Example: Process flow weekly planning

Daily planning is the process to plan daily vehicle production considering latest contraction and sudden events. Daily planning confirms sequence target orders. By re-planning weekly plan reflecting latest contracted orders and weekly plan's guide which cannot be violated, the solution can cope with emergency order and customer requirement change efficiently. Daily planning should provide vehicle stock reduction and production stability by rapid re-planning.

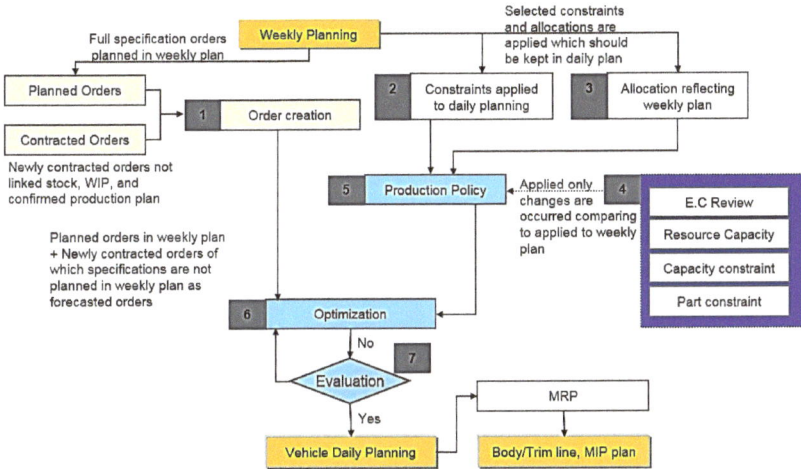

Example: Process flow Daily Planning

Demand Management – Components

The first major element of the SAP solution architecture is the decision not to explode the full spec vehicle in the SAP systems. In order to provide a plant with the information it requires to execute the assembly process and to address the material management requirements two data flows are provided by the head office: Component and Vehicle.

Based on monthly/weekly planning a MRP run generates the requirements for all relevant components for the defined time period. This information is fed into the SD module of the SAP system. This interface provides the functionality required for the spare part process. The incoming demand is verified. Errors, Warnings and information are logged and forwarded to an Alert Monitor. In the monitor tolerances are defined, such that should the demand deviate a record is written into the log.

Incoming demand is released automatically. Various alerts can stop the release – which than requires a manual release. A single MRP run will generate the demand required to generate the schedules for all component suppliers. Depending on the type of part/supply strategy this schedule is used be suppliers as either for planning purposes and or as delivery schedule. JIT suppliers will receive an additional message which will be discussed later. This approach will allow to establish a fully functional supply chain.

Demand Management – Vehicle

Weekly/daily vehicle demand including a resolved BOM for each vehicle / JIT parts is sent to the SAP system on a regular basis. This information is interpreted as a JIT inbound message, with an attached BOM for all JIT components. The JIT BOM can be transmitted with the vehicle order, however is also stored in the SAP system. Since the JIT components are assembled in various stations they are equipped with a time stamp. This is done based on component based lead time and time from the vehicle sequence. The respective suppliers is given information about the configuration of each vehicle, vehicle number, time stamp, sequence number etc. For each component or group, a point is defined at which the respective signal for the JIT message is generated.

4.5 Vehicle Assembly/Manufacturing

The scope of the vehicle manufacturing section covers the four major processes:

- Stamping
- Body Assembly
- Paint Shop
- Trim

In house manufacturing involving blanking, stamping operation producing A,B or C parts. Some B and C parts are outsourced to local suppliers. The required coil material is stored with $10 - 20$ days inventory in order to guarantee uninterrupted operation. The local output will be stored in a storage system from which the body operation draws the required parts. The outsourced parts from external suppliers made available via storage with several hours' capacity. The entire stamping operation is implemented in SAP as a separate plant. The remaining operations body, paint and assembly are supported by dedicated solutions.

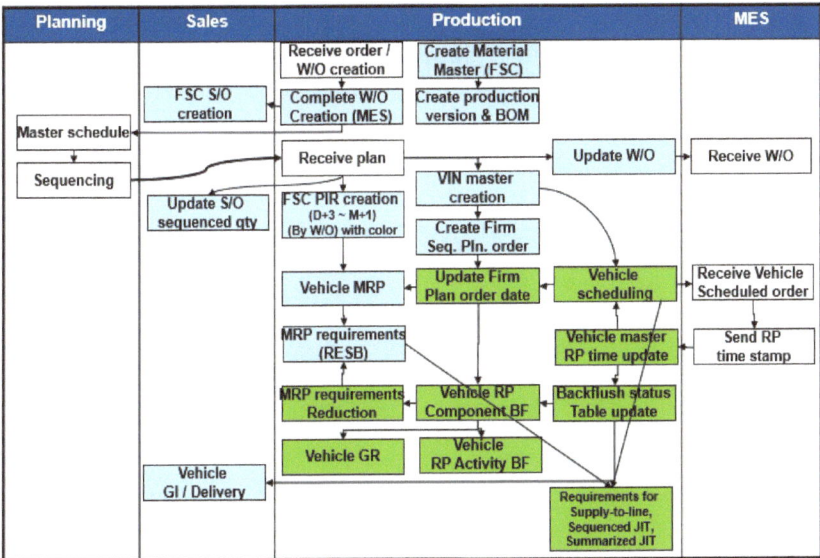

Planning	Sales	Production		MES
		Receive order / W/O creation	Create Material Master (FSC)	
	FSC S/O creation	Complete W/O Creation (MES)	Create production version & BOM	
Master schedule		Receive plan		
Sequencing			VIN master creation	Update W/O	Receive W/O
	Update S/O sequenced qty	FSC PIR creation (D+3 ~ M+1) (By W/O) with color	Create Firm Seq. Pln. order	
		Vehicle MRP	Update Firm Plan order date	Vehicle scheduling	Receive Vehicle Scheduled order
		MRP requirements (RESB)		Vehicle master RP time update	Send RP time stamp
		MRP requirements Reduction	Vehicle RP Component BF	Backflush status Table update	
		Vehicle GR	Vehicle RP Activity BF		
	Vehicle GI / Delivery		Requirements for Supply-to-line, Sequenced JIT, Summarized JIT	

Stamping – Press Shop

In the stamping department, that is fully integrated into SAP, long rolls of coiled steel are cut into sections (blanks) in the Blanking Line in preparation to be formed. The forming process is completed when the blanks are automatically inserted into a stamping press between an upper and lower die. The performance of the stamping press is of high production volume per hour in high speed and exerts thousands of pounds of force onto the sheet of steel to form it into a part. Major panels such as skin and bigger-sized panels are manufactured inside the plant (MIP parts) and delivered to the Welding Shop automatically by Electro Mono Rails(EMS) to be assembled into the car body in white. Many of the sheet metal parts that are used to piece together the vehicles will be made in the stamping department. SAP is using Make-To-Stock (MTS) with production orders to be able to control the stamping process in detail.

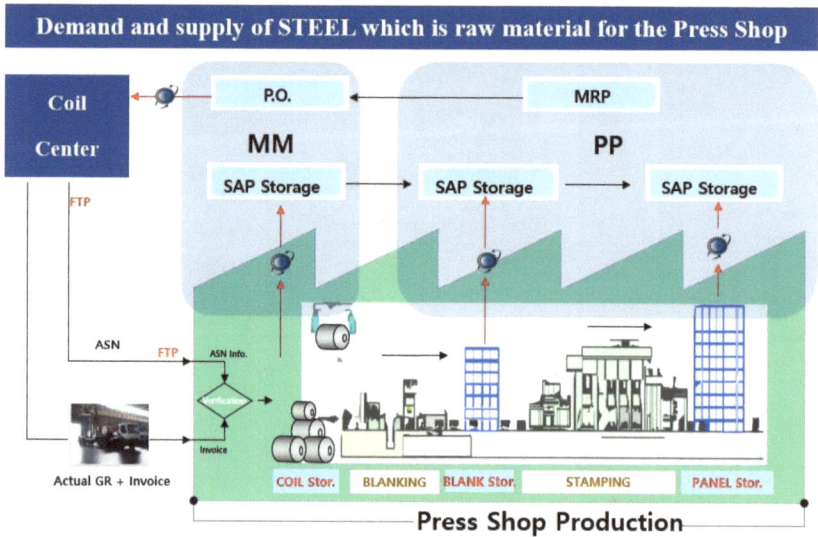

Demand and supply of STEEL which is raw material for the Press Shop

Press Shop Production

STEEL's Material Master is created normally by the Catalog; once Production department forms Blank Master, it identifies matching materials. When no matching material is found, STEEL Material number is empty at this point a possible match can be identified by manually selecting the closest material.

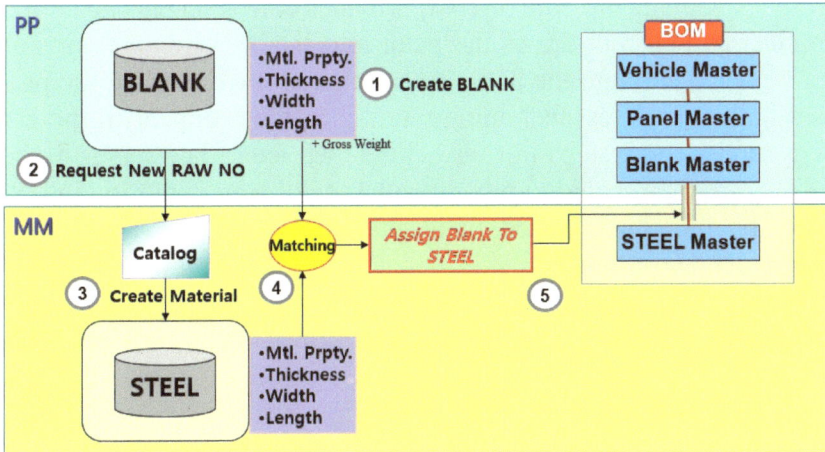

Welding (Body Shop)

In the welding department, the pieces of metal are put together. It is here that the shape of the vehicle comes together. Precision accuracy of these components is required so that all dimensions on the vehicle are within tight specifications. The vehicle is assembled in several stages. First, the underbody and front structure are built. While the underbody and floor pan are being assembled, the body sides of the vehicle are assembled. These parts, along with the roof, come together in the framing fixture, and the shell of the vehicle is formed. The closure panels (hood, doors, deck lid) are then attached to the vehicle to complete the building process. Finally, the vehicle is inspected for metal finish smoothness to ensure a dent free vehicle.

Painting (Paint Shop)

In the paint department, coatings are applied to the body to prevent rust and add the color to the vehicle. The body is first put through a cleaning process followed by the application of a zinc phosphate coating that will allow the water-based undercoat to adhere perfectly. A cathode dip bath (e-coat) provides corrosion resistance and an electrical current draws the paint into the most remote parts of the vehicle. Through the 360-degree rotation movement in the process baths, the latest technology, no air bubbles appear in the car body cavity and less paint runs behind the e-coat. The seams of the vehicle are then sealed to prevent any type of water entering into it. After the underbody protection is applied, the body moves to a drying tunnel. Once the vehicle is e-coated and sealed, it is primed and then painted with a topcoat and clear coat of paint. High-speed atomizers provide an ultra-fine mist, drawn onto the body by electrostatic charging to give smoothest possible finish. The final topcoat is applied and hardened in a drying oven. The vehicle is then inspected under high level, intense lighting to ensure there are no imperfections in the finish.

General Assembly (Trim Shop)

In the general assembly department, all components necessary to finish the vehicle are assembled. Everything from the electrical components to the engine and tires are put on the vehicles on the conveyor. Work is done in many stations which are designed for high productivity, strict quality orientation, the highest level of flexibility and exemplary ergonomic standards. At the end of this process, the vehicles are ready to be tested before being delivered to consumers. Many kinds of tests, such as dynamic vehicle tests and road tests, are performed in dynamic conditions, and other static tests are performed by reliable, high-tech test machines. All tests are performed on all aspects of the vehicle to ensure quality and reliability. SAP is heavily involved by using a fast performance calculation to support the production supply into so called Production Supply Areas (PSA). These works with a real time connection into the production line, to inform SAP precisely about the vehicle status and process. SAP calculates an expected workstation passing time, so that these workstations on the line can be supplied with only parts that are needed for vehicles that will pass in an hour.

Body-, Paint- and Trim Shop are all connected through one production line and controlled with SAP together with real time connection to Manufacturing Execution System (MES) and Assembly Line Control (MES). A Make-To-Order (MTO) is used to drive sales orders over planning, MRP into production. Mass production completion per vehicle for each reporting point (auto-ID) are used to keep track of the vehicle and supporting production supply. The challenge of extreme mass data volume will be mastered by a specific rapid backflush.

Example: Supply Chain flow from Order, Vendor, ship into production warehouse, supply to line process

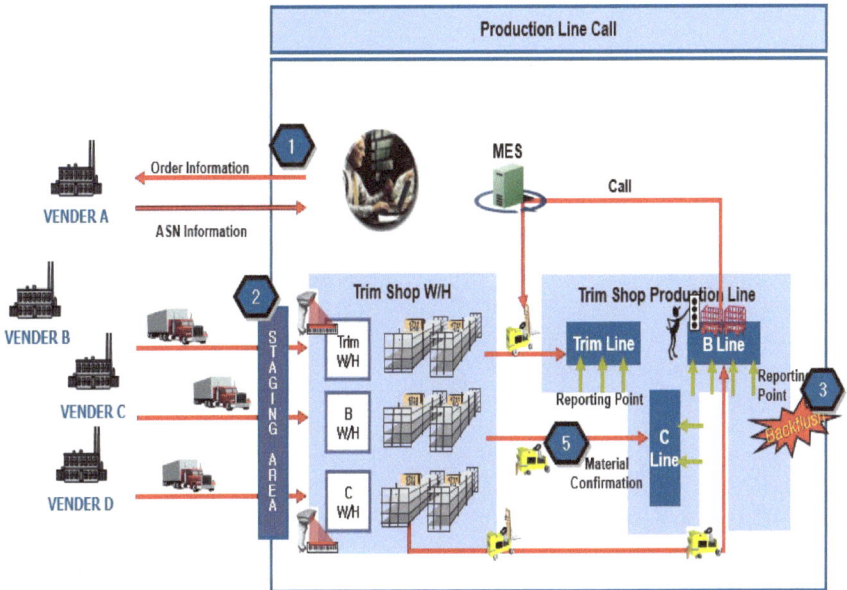

Engine production – Engine shop

The engine shop is the area where the raw materials are placed on a machining line and assembled into parts - cylinder blocks, cylinder heads and crank shafts - with local parts. The engine shop consists of multiple machining lines and one assembly line to make engines. The engine design is created by unique technology and produce different types of engines. On the machining line, each part is input as raw material status and machined one by one according to the part's specification, and then the quality control division checks its machining status. In order to produce engine parts effectively, the "Agile" production system is applied.

The engine assembly line uses high technology test equipment to check the engine parts assembling status. After all the parts are assembled, the engine will be tested on two kinds of engine assembly test equipment - cold test bench and hot test bench.

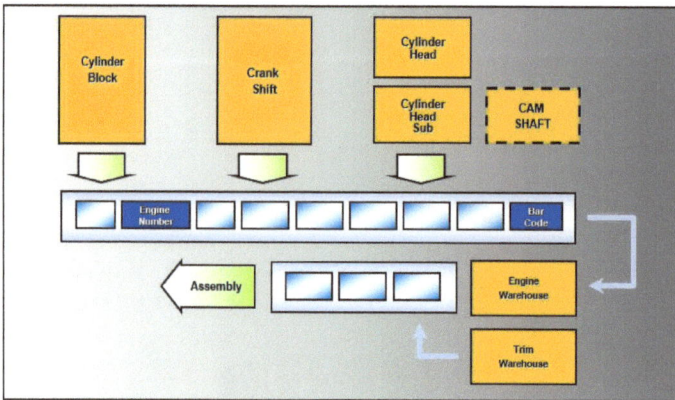

Production Control

In the production control department using SAP for the whole supply chain activities, beginning with the sales order, receiving parts from suppliers and manufacturers, and delivery to dealers. It is important to visualize information and control each chain.

The focus is on production in order "to provide products that sell" to the end customer market. This is achieved by its primary goal of demand driven structure with improving production effectiveness in its myriad forms, such as flexibility, quick responsiveness, productivity, and profitability as follows:

- An SAP system that provides advanced business processing connected in real time to an Advanced Planning and Scheduling (APS) system for production operation, parts supply and sales visibilities
- An in-house production information system Assembly Line Control (MES) and a Manufacturing Execution System(MES) for raising productivity
- A Logistics Management System (LMS) for the process of planning, implementing and controlling the efficient, cost effective flow and storage of raw materials, in-process inventory, finished goods, and related information from point-of-origin to point-of-consumption for the purpose of confirming customer requirements.

Production Backflush

Parts relief is performed real time for parts that where inventory accuracy is key and at the end of each shift in batch mode. Hence, inventory levels shown in the system are real-time or up to one shift old. In order to support business requirement for 'near real-time' inventory, real-time consumption is implemented with the SAP solution. The SAP system supports this functionality which has initially being developed.

Followed by the Vehicle Manufacturing process and upon SAP planned order creation, the consumption/backflush process is ready for execution once:

- The time stamp/event in which consumption is due to be executed (e.g. consumption at predefined action points*) has been identified

- When an action point, which can trigger events such as material relief, has been reached

- It has been determined where and when parts fitted at multiple line locations are due to be consumed

- Checkpoints have been related to action points (e.g. end of body-in-white is assigned to an action point triggering consumption of all parts fitted to the vehicle in Body-shop)

- Action points have been allocated to material components

- Planned Orders have been populated with the BOM explosion result

- Aggregated backflush reduces the amount of material documents to be posted and is hence, less performance critical. The consumption postings are carried out during production and therefore support 3-shift operations.

- The handling of negative inventory (e.g. as a typical result of bad timing between the actual receiving of the goods and the posting of the goods issue of the materials) is addressed by allowing negative inventory on the PSA (Production Supply Area).

Vehicle Issue into Sales

The vehicle issue process is the last step of the integrated process chain. Upon delivery of the vehicle to the sales organization, the cycle for the core process vehicle is closed. At the time a finished vehicle drops off line, it is placed into plant stock. Afterwards, the vehicle can be issued to the Customer/Dealer. For customs and financial reporting, it will be necessary that the Planned Orders is kept in the SAP system. The BOM and costs is stored in the backflush tables for a specified retention period. The final step is to invoice the vehicle to the Customer or Sales Organization after it passed the "money gate".

Engine Assembly/Sales Order

The engine plant is set up as a supplier to the assemble plant for engines and supplier of spare parts. The plant receives long term planning information and sales orders for engines and engine parts. The engines are drawn from the engine storage based on the information from the assembly line. The actual production of the engines is driven by the SAP solution. The SAP solution is also responsible for the generation of the secondary demand. The secondary demand drives the schedules for the engine plan suppliers. At the end of the production run, are the engines stored.

The incoming sequence signal triggers a SAP JIT process that generates a production order. The last manufacturing step triggers a back flash of all used components.
Each engine receives a unique assembly/engine number. The primary demand for spare parts is added to the secondary demand generated by the MRP run. In order to supply material to the assembly line scenarios like Kanban are used in some areas.

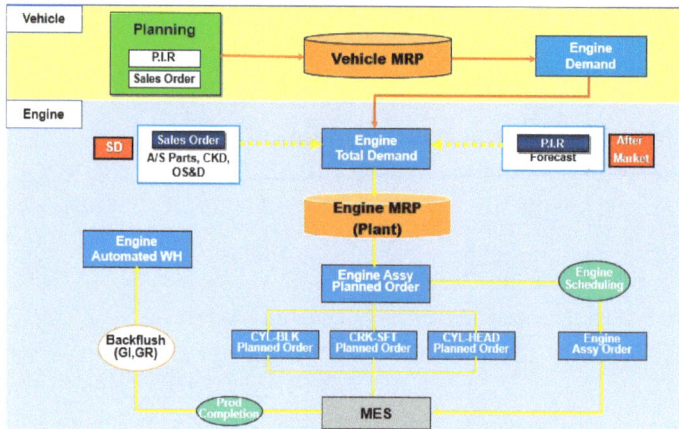

Example: Integration between Vehicle and Engine Planning

4.6 Material Planning

Material Planning process converts the demand data into actual requirements for parts. Production requirements for finished goods drive requirements for subassemblies and components through the explosion of the bill of material at all levels. Requirements for internal production move to production control to monitor and update detailed scheduling, while external requirements are sent to suppliers and tracked to the point of receipt. Requirements for parts are driven for warranty commitments and spare parts sales.

As a high level breakdown for Vehicle Assembly area, the following material types are used for material planning after the BOM explosion is completed for sequenced vehicle models: (In sequence of material flow)
- Coils
- Parts for Body Assembly
  - In-house Produced
  - Externally Procured
- Vehicle Assembly Line Parts
  - JIT Parts
  - JIS Parts

As a high level breakdown for Engine Assembly area, the following material types are used for material planning:(In sequence of material flow)

- Ingots
- In-house manufactured machining parts
- In-house manufactured assembly parts
- Transmissions and other parts that are imported
- Externally procured components

All of these parts require different planning horizons such as monthly, daily or just-in-time. They also require different strategies in order to plan shipments accurately and decrease the level of inventory that is required to run the manufacturing operations at a desired service level.

Importing – Foreign Trade Zone

A Foreign-Trade Zone (FTZ) is a specially designated area, in or adjacent to a U.S. Customs port of Entry, which is considered to be outside the customs territory of the U.S. Subzones are special-purpose zones, usually at manufacturing plants.

The Customs Service is responsible for the transfer of merchandise into and out of a zone and for matters involving the collection of revenue.

Zones are supervised by U.S. Customs officers through periodic checks and visits; the security of the zone must meet U.S. Customs requirements

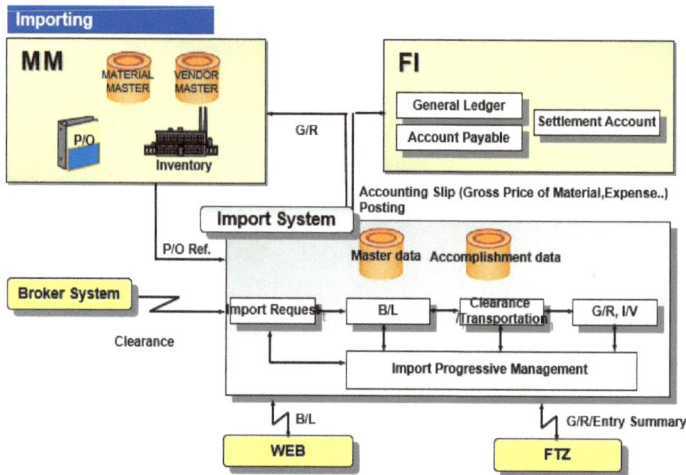

Importing

MM
MATERIAL MASTER   VENDOR MASTER
P/O
Inventory

G/R

FI
General Ledger
Settlement Account
Account Payable

Accounting Slip (Gross Price of Material, Expense..)
Posting

Import System

P/O Ref.

Master data   Accomplishment data

Broker System

Import Request   B/L   Clearance /Transportation   G/R, I/V

Clearance

Import Progressive Management

B/L

G/R/Entry Summary

WEB

FTZ

Material Planning / MRP

MRP forms a vital part of the logistics process for the manufacturing and assembly of vehicles. By ensuring a smooth material flow to meet the part requirements, MRP helps to guarantee material availability. Part requirements are used to procure or produce the required quantities on time both for internal purposes and for Sales and Distribution.

The process involves the monitoring of stocks and, in particular, the automatic creation of procurement proposals for purchasing and production (Planned Orders, Purchase requisitions, Schedule lines). Based on the parameters and strategies adopted, MRP provides a delivery schedules for the supply of externally procured parts to production. The MRP material master consists of parameters that control planning, consuming and issuing of materials.

Material planning is based on dealer forecasts and firmed dealer orders (sales orders) for vehicles. MRP calculation in SAP has a direct dependency on these demands. MRP also considers in-transit quantities which are tracked based on Advance Shipping Notification (ASN). In addition, the automotive business requirement to differentiate plant inventory per storage location is supported.

MRP supports the concept of negative inventory, as well as exclusion of certain identified storage locations in the net calculation. However, negative system inventory will be immediately reordered once MRP runs, possibly causing discrepancies between planned and actual requirements.

MRP takes into account inventories, expected receipts, safety stock levels and lot-sizes of materials. In addition to outputs such as procurement proposals, Exceptions Messages are created which allows the Planners to analyze the situation with respect to materials' availability for production. MRP runs take into consideration the Engineering Change Requests that will become valid in the future to apply the changes to future procurement requests.

Example: Planned Orders (firmed) are sequenced through the different shops

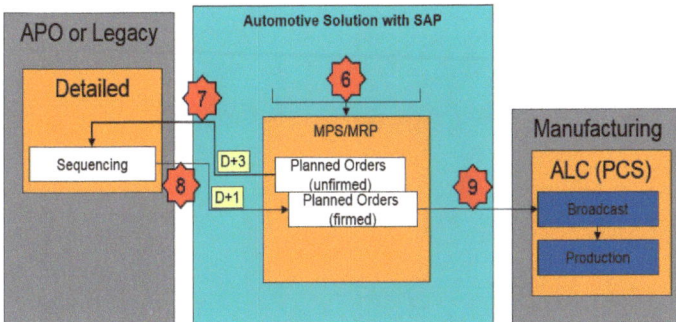

The Broadcast system is responsible to deliver the required production information to the vehicle line. The output from the demand management (=independent requirements) is used as input for the MRP run of finished goods. At a certain point in time actual day plus three days (D+3) only sales orders have to be considered by the MRP run. At this point in time, the independent requirements are deleted. The MPS/MRP run creates planned orders and if Sales Order exist, a planned orders will inherit the characteristics (configuration). Planned Orders within the horizon of x days (D+3) are send to sequencing.

Example: Sequencing of vehicles and adding the VIN number

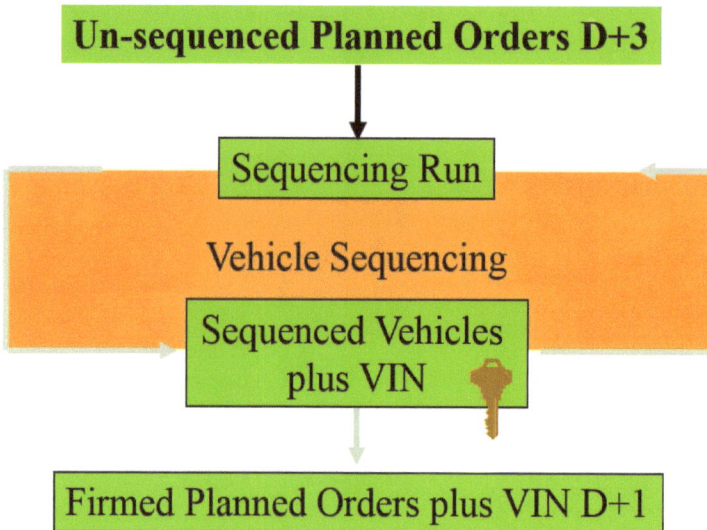

Un-sequenced Planned Orders D+3

Sequencing Run

Vehicle Sequencing

Sequenced Vehicles plus VIN

Firmed Planned Orders plus VIN D+1

VIN # is assigned and sequenced planned orders will be firmed in SAP to protect against changes.

Model Mix Planning (MMP)

The Model Mix Planning process consists of the following major areas:

- Model Mix planning and master data
- Sequencing
- Restrictions
- Takt-based scheduling

Model Mix Planning is used for takt-based flow manufacturing of configured products. MMP optimizes the sequence of orders by considering daily volumes or shift packages and is suited for the demand of large order volumes. Vehicles that are often configured are produced together on one production line. In model mix planning determines an order sequence with start and end dates, which fulfills specific business aims, taking restrictions and customers' preferred dates into account. This will be, for example, the following:

- An equal load of the line segments or takt's
- A minimization of restriction violations
- A minimization of the absolute schedule deviation

Model Mix Planning allows the definition of different planning horizons and has an automatic planning run over a specific period. The Model Mix Planning is a part of the APO PP/DS module or it can also be supported using an external system interfaced into SAP and is based on the master data of the line design function.

The number and the length of the horizons, as well as the procedures to be used can be defined individually. In the long to medium-term area, orders can be assigned to only one period slot, whilst in the short-term area, complex sequencing that includes all restrictions can be carried out. Depending on system settings, the system only uses existing planned orders, or also converts customer orders and planned independent requirements into planned orders.

Equal models are produced on production lines and the model mix planning allows you to set up the planned order sequence and line selections with start and end dates based on restrictions. As some example restrictions could be set for a minimum of violations, a minimum of scheduled deviation or takt time loads.

The different planning horizons are defined as:

- Long-term planning: the goal is to get a 100%-line load and plan with summarized planned orders.
- Medium-term planning: the goal is to create pre-sequence and plan with the defined quantity restrictions.
- Short-term planning: the goal is the final detailed sequence. Plan with all defined restrictions and detailed requested dates from the market demand. Period, mostly this is for a week.

The model mix planning will run every day based on the input from sales or ad hoc based on manual adjustments made or required. The planning result is displayed in the product-planning table where you have the overview of the planned orders on a shift or daily base.

The APO system will convert planned independent requirements into planned orders and uses planned orders for the model mix planning. Period Leveling can be used in the Medium-term periods to create a 100% load of each period. The model mix planning will be generating new planned orders or move them from one period to another based on constraints. Planned order quantities are required not to be scheduled out in the future past the requirements date as customer commitments have been based on the requirements dates.

Sequencing – Sequenced schedule

The sequence schedule is used to display, evaluate and process the results of model mix planning. It represents the sequence of APO orders for a planned version and line structure. Functionality to check the quality of the sequence by means of showing any restriction violations is also provided.

The sequencing and optimizing will only be used for the short-term horizon. The sequencing result can be changed manually if necessary to cover any unplanned event. Optimal sequencing can be done when lot sizes of 1 are used (one planned order covers 1 vehicle).

Scheduling Restrictions

Restrictions are conditions to be taken into account by the planning process when optimizing the order sequence. Restrictions are the "rules and regulation" of the line sequencing to ensure an optimum load of personnel and machines as well as to guarantee the availability of materials. You can define so called hard and soft restrictions. Hard restrictions cannot be violated, for example, the fully automated paint process is restricted by the maximum quantity (capacity) per hour. Soft restrictions can be violated and are managed by prioritize the restriction in important and not so important. Or in other words soft restrictions with a very low priority will probably violated. The exact restrictions will be defined in the merge/diverge design.

Restrictions are used for the definition of conditions for the occurrence of characteristic values in a planning period. There are currently six restriction categories supported in APO PP/DS:

- Quantity restriction
- Spacing restriction
- Block restriction
- K-in-M restriction (minimum or maximum quantity in a certain interval) e.g.: three out of five products must have the same attributes
- Position restriction (to limit the occurrence of certain combinations)
- Event distribution (to evenly distribute certain combinations of characteristics over a certain period) e.g.: a maximum of 150 vehicles can only be built with air-conditioning per shift

The restrictions are then taken into account in Model Mix Planning to calculate an optimal order sequence.

Takt based Scheduling

Takt-based scheduling is a type of scheduling, which is specially used for takt-based production lines. As model mix planning is intended for planning takt-based production lines, you can only work with takt-based scheduling here. The system

Object	Node	Category	Elements	Description & etc.
Line design	Line	Capacity	Calendar	Work calendar definition
		UPH	Maximum UPH	Unit per Hours
			Periodic plan UPH	
	Shop	Scheduling capacity	Calendar	Work calendar definition (IMG)
			Periodic working hour per shift	Shift definition (IMG)
	Reporting Point	Tack	No of tack (= estimated no of cars from RP to next RP)	Minimum 1 (for T24 sign-off)
Reference rate routing	Operation	Sequence of operation (RP)	OP no with RP as a work center	0010 B01, 0020 P02, ...
		Backflush points	Control key	BFNO for RP without backflush BFPT for backflush point
		Supply area		Supply to Line

does not calculate the lead time of an order from the duration of the activities, but by multiplying the number of takts with the takt time. Therefore, the takt time is the reciprocal of the rate.

Takt-BASED scheduling can only take place if all orders are based on the quantity. Unlike model mix planning, takt-based scheduling does take breaks into account Takt-based scheduling is based on the master data of the linc design. Here you can divide your line into line segments over as many hierarchy levels as you wish, and group several lines to line networks.

Vehicle Variant Structure

The product variant concept has been used in SAP for many years. The concept is to have a structure defined that includes all of the possible characteristics for a product. The product's available colors and sizes would certainly be included, along with any other features that the customer is allowed to choose from. The structure includes restrictions such as the external color combined with internal color. The structure also includes dependencies such as the engine size drives the battery size. The end result is that this one structure can be used to configure the end product exactly as the customer wants it.

The structure can be used by itself, but then all orders are customer specific and are generally only built when an order exists. The product variant structure could be used directly to support the constrained build to order model (CBTO). The structure can also be used to create variants that are a unique combination of the characteristics in the structure. These are called material variants. A product variant structure would represent all the possible features of a specific model code, while a material variant would be a let say black model with air conditioning, gray leather interior, Radio with cd-player, Sport version etc. These variants would allow the planning and scheduling of the specific types of models being built regardless of whether or not a sales order existed.

Procurement Purchasing – Parts Ordering

Due to the strong dependencies between Purchasing and Material Planning, purchasing relevant master data as described below is a prerequisite to support an integrated procurement process. The SAP Purchasing module controls the method of supplier communication as well as various methods for procurement. The necessary master data elements are Material Master, Vendor Master, Source list and Quota arrangements and others. Material master records contain all the necessary information about a purchased material or planned delivery time. Vendor master records contain all the information about a vendor/supplier such as name, address, and terms of payments, but also communication control parameters for the transmission of delivery schedules. Every time a material is planned by MRP, the source list is being read in order to determine the applicable vendor and scheduling agreement for procurement. Quota arrangements have to be maintained for materials sourced from multiple vendors at the same time.

Parts Order Planning, has two components: Mid-term and Sub-daily (Daily Ordering System). All suppliers receive a release from the Weekly Result. The release is to be the forecast, or long-term planning document. Fabrication and raw material authorizations are issued from this result and daily receipt for suppliers RE are created that deliver only once per day. Most long lead-time suppliers receive their schedule from it.

APO Rapid Planning Matrix (RPM) functionality in conjunction with SAP R/3 MRP and KANBAN functions can be used for above described parts order planning processes.
APO to plan component requirements for the final assembly of products with many variants and large numbers of orders. It is part of Model Mix Planning (MMP) in APO to generate planned orders for the sales orders, to determine the sequence of the planned orders on the production line, and the start and end dates for the planned orders. The component requirements are scheduled in the rapid planning matrix based on the order start dates.

The components that are to be planned in APO are planned using production planning and detailed scheduling. You can continue planning for other components in the ECC system. The planning file entries for these components are transferred to the ECC system and planned using MRP and KANBAN. This enables you to take the load off APO without losing the advantages of the quick explosion in the matrix.

Process Flow
- Order demand into APO.
- Planning run using Model Mix Planning
- Creates planned orders and assigns them to a predefined production line
- Creation of the Rapid Planning Matrix
- Sequence planned orders

- System explodes the product variant structure for APO orders and creates dependent requirements for components (15 minute buckets)
- Dependent requirements for components are sent from APO to R/3 via CIF
- Supply to Line does calculation
- Reads the APO Matrix to calculate the requirements
- Reads the sequence
- Looks at reporting point in line design to determine when component is required at the line
- Summarized JIT call for component created

Additionally, purchasing information records are set up as a central source of information for Purchasing. Unlike purchase orders for one time buys, scheduling agreements are used as long-term agreements with vendors for material purchases. MRP generated schedule lines are automatically transferred into scheduling agreements and represent the delivery schedule.

The scheduling agreement also consists of pricing relevant information, as well as the history of goods received and previous delivery schedules transmitted. Schedule agreements can be setup for regular deliveries or JIT based on the material and the supply area of the material that is consumed. The closing of one time shipments upon material receiving in case of over- or under deliveries are parameterized in the SAP system. In other words, a delivery schedule being under delivered does not automatically close the planned shipment in the Scheduling agreement. This process is to be designed with special attention since over- and under delivery scenarios can lead to major discrepancies for Material Planning.

Vendor evaluation functionality in SAP will allow to evaluate the performance of the vendor based on them on time, accurate delivery, and other industry-wide standard metrics that can be defined in SAP. SAP Inbound Logistics functionalities such as ASN, is utilized to monitor the shipments from suppliers. Tracking of shipments via several tracking points allow to manage the estimated times of the shipments better and respond the delays before they occur.

SAP Invoice Verification functionality, such Evaluated Receipt Settlement (ERS), is used to automate the payment procedures where possible. This functionality not only streamlines the process but also improves the error handling with the suppliers.

Standard Parts Ordering

Standard parts are materials that are used on every vehicle made of a particular model. All fasteners are in this category of materials; nuts, bolts, screws, clips, etc. Also in this group are caps, covers, protective bushing, etc. All of the parts are ordered mainly from the same vendor. Typically, they are small parts of low cost, used in multiple applications at multiple points along the assembly line. This relationship is represented by the quantity required, in total, per vehicle. In SAP, the quantity required per vehicle will be reflected in a phantom BOM. A Kanban process can be used to replenish the parts. The general process for ordering, receiving, and managing standard parts would also be changed, to reduce the amount of on-hand inventory and to create a consignment situation, instead of having the plant own the standard parts inventory.

Process

- Forecast release is created and sent to vendor for planning purposes
- Estimated demand for a time period is calculated periodically for a period of time
- Vendor creates shipment and sends ASN
- Multiple physical carts will be used for each line-side cart location. Some will be at line-side, and the others will be at the vendor warehouse. The vendor will restock the cart, wait for the cycle time to elapse, and deliver the refilled cart to the plant.

- Processing the ASN and receives the material into consignment inventory. The carts are delivered to the line side location. The other carts will be taken from line-side and returned to the vendor.
- The material is owned by the vendor until backflush occurs and the goods issue for the standard part causes a reduction of the consignment inventory and creation of an accounts payable liability.

Bulk Material Ordering

There are multiple hundreds of bulk materials in a vehicle for example lubricants, adhesives, sealers, and oil and gas. The bulk materials can be represented in the vehicle BOM, but indicated as bulk part. Under a phantom parent material for grouping purposes, each bulk material is listed with its usage per hour. The shop calendar is used to calculate the hours worked per day. These hours per day are loaded to the forecast of the bulk material parent part.

Because they are not in the vehicle BOM identified as production relevant (bulk parts), inventory relief for bulk materials is not accomplished when vehicle production is reported. A cycle count of bulk materials is taken. The purpose is to attain accurate inventory quantities. These quantities can be collected by many different methods. Inventory of each bulk material number is adjusted. MRP is executed for the parent bulk material, and the quantity required for each bulk material is calculated per day. The remaining net requirements are used to create the forecast release. These requirements are shown as daily requirements.

Each bulk material is purchased with a purchasing blanket order (schedule agreement). The requirements are automatically loaded to the blanket order for this material. Each day is a separate requirement. The bulk material may be used in one unit of measure but purchased in another. Common conversions within a class of measures (weight, volume, area, or distance) are known to SAP.

Special conversions can be defined. Two outputs will be created from this process:

- Forecast Release: The process of taking these daily requirements and accumulating them into daily, weekly, and monthly totals. For example, the release creation can describe that for the first 3 weeks send daily totals; for the following 10 weeks send weekly totals; and for the following 3 months send monthly totals. It also identified the horizon (total number of days) to be sent in the release. The release creation parameters can be unique to a material / supplier combination.

New shipment authorizations are created for a short-term horizon. These Summarized JIT Calls can be lot sized to the standard pack received. Example: a tanker of 30,000 pounds.

Engineering Change Management - ECM

Changes planned and executed in the design are applied to the BOM. These changes are incorporated to SAP via the ECM release process using OCM (Order Change Management). Before the physical change occurs in SAP OCM will be used to identify any impact on the currently running production line and required steps will take place in order to process what and where a change can be applied.

ECM is embedded into DMS (Document Management System) for engineering specs, drawings, operational instructions, quality inspection results and other documents, as well as for routings, BOMs and material master changes.

4.7 Material Supply on the Production Line

There are various options for **controlling** the **material flow** of components to your production lines planning-based, using the **pull list,** consumption-based, using **storage location MRP and KANBAN**.

With the use of KANBAN, production is <u>not</u> planned by a planning department or planner on an on-going basis. Instead, production of a material is initiated when it is needed by the next higher manufacturing level. When the inventory of the KANBAN product gets low at the demand source (i.e., the next higher level in the production process), replenishment by the supply source is triggered. When demand ceases at the demand source, there is no further production at the supply source. Production of a KANBAN material is not initiated in anticipation of demand, but rather as a direct result of actual demand.

Controlling Material Flow

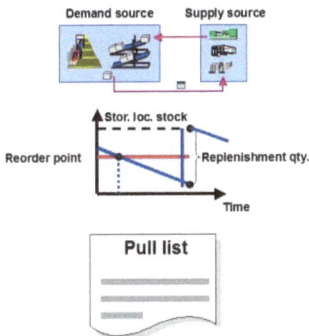

1 ● KANBAN

2 ● Consumption-based
(storage location MRP)

3 ● Planning-based
(pull list)

KANBAN

In KANBAN, material flow is organized using containers which are kept directly at the appropriate work centers in production. Each contains the quantity of material that work center personnel need for a certain period of time. As soon as a container is emptied at the demand source, replenishment is initiated. The supply source for the required material can be another place in production, an external supplier or a warehouse. The demand source can use material from buffer containers until the actual container returns to full.

The aim of the KANBAN system is to control the production process from production itself, and to reduce the manual tasks required of personnel. This self-management and the fact that replenishment elements are created close to the time they are actually consumed means that stocks are reduced (replenishment is only triggered when a material is actually required and not before) and lead times shortened.

KANBAN in summary: material is staged where it is used. It remains there, in small material buffers, ready for use. Thus, material staging does not need to be planned. Instead, material that is consumed is replenished immediately using KANBAN.

If you use KANBAN alongside the R/3 System, you can automate the transmission of replenishment data. This means that scanning the barcode on the KANBAN card is enough to transmit the data needed for procurement and to post the goods receipt upon receipt of the material. With KANBAN, material is staged where it is used. It remains there, in small buffers, ready for use. Thus, material staging does not need to be planned. Instead, material that is consumed is replenished immediately using KANBAN.

If KANBAN is implemented with the support of the R/3 system, transmission of replenishment data can be automated: scanning the barcode on the Kanban card suffices to transmit the data needed for procurement and to post the goods receipt upon receipt of the material.

KANBAN

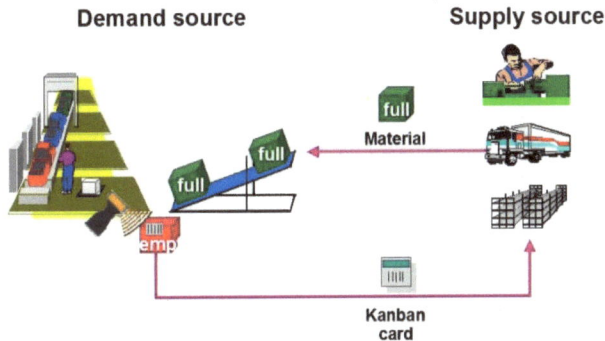

Should the supply source be a production line, a run schedule quantity can be created by setting the KANBAN to "empty" and can be confirmed using the "final backflush for KANBAN".

Storage Location MRP / Reorder Point

Material requirements planning is usually carried out at plant level, but **storage location MRP** is also possible. This means that the MRP run plans material requirements specifically for the flagged storage location.

Storage location MRP uses **manual reorder point planning** at the storage location level. To enable storage location MRP, the *MRP indicator 2* in the material master must be set for a certain storage location, causing that storage location's stock requirements to be planned separately. A *reorder point* and a *replenishment quantity* must also be defined for the material at the storage location. Storage location stock can therefore be monitored automatically; when it falls below the reorder point, it is automatically replenished. The system generates an order

Storage Location MRP

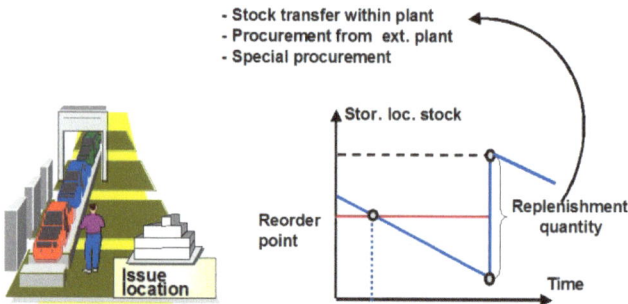

proposal corresponding to the replenishment quantity, or a whole multiple of the replenishment quantity, in order to bring the total stock at the storage location greater than the reorder point. Inward movements that already exist for the warehouse are taken into account when this is performed (as with reorder point procedures at plant level). Stock in a storage location that is planned separately is not included in the available stock at plant level.

Storage location stock that is planned separately can be procured in different ways, **Stock transfers within a plant** from storage locations that are not planned separately. **Special procurement for the storage location that is planned separately**. This means that external or internal procurement can be directly triggered for this special storage location and **Procurement from another plant**.

Warehouse Management & Pull list using PSA (Production Supply Area)

This is the most accurate supply replenishment, however it requires exact data to run correctly. The pull list controls the internal material flow of supplies to production. It is assumed that the components required by production have already been produced in-house or procured externally, and now simply have to be transferred from their current storage location or bin to the supply area (**internal material staging**). The pull list checks the component stock situation at the production storage location (issue storage location) and compares it to the requirements situation from the master plan (**material staging based on planning**). The calculated difference equals the missing parts. Replenishment elements can be created for these missing parts. One method of staging components is **direct stock transfer** in which the system posts the goods issue of the components from the replenishment storage location. A list of these

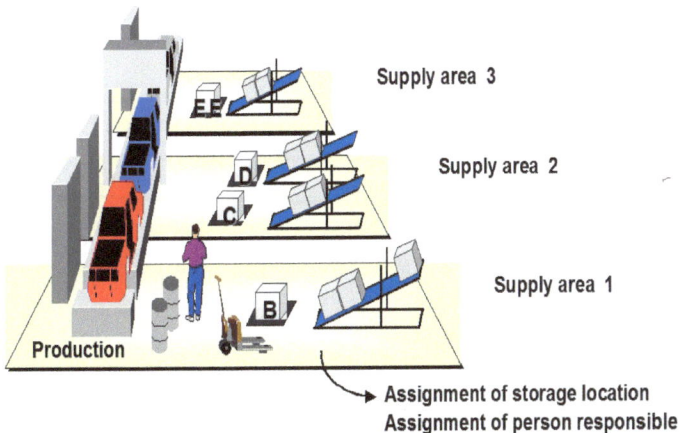

Supply area 3

Supply area 2

Supply area 1

Production

Assignment of storage location
Assignment of person responsible

postings may be printed for warehouse personnel. This list states the replenishment location, the target storage location and the quantity required, and can then be used to carry out the physical stock transfer.

There are **Prerequisites,** the issue storage location for the components must already be known. That is, the dependent requirements must already be storage location specific since the pull list displays only those requirements for which the issue storage location has already been specified. The issue storage location can be specified at the material master of the component, at the item level in the BOM of the assembly, or in the production version of the assembly.

Pull List With Direct Transfer Posting

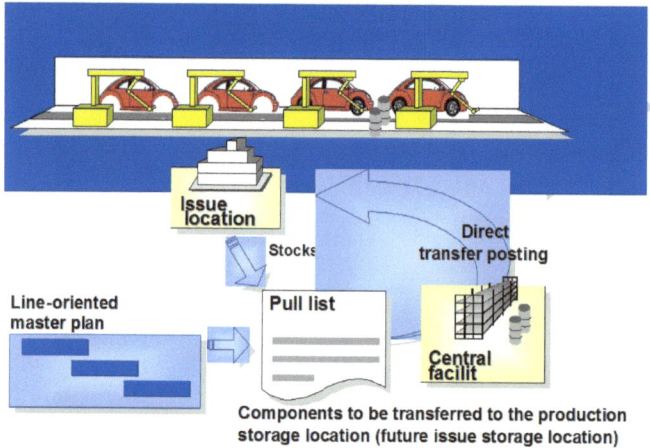

Issue location

Stocks

Direct transfer posting

Line-oriented master plan

Pull list

Central facilit

Components to be transferred to the production storage location (future issue storage location)

The pull list controls the in-house flow of material for supplying production with materials. The system assumes that the components required for production have already been produced in-house or procured externally and are now available to be transferred from their current storage location or bin to the production storage location.

The pull list checks the stock situation at the production storage location and calculates the quantities of missing parts. Replenish-

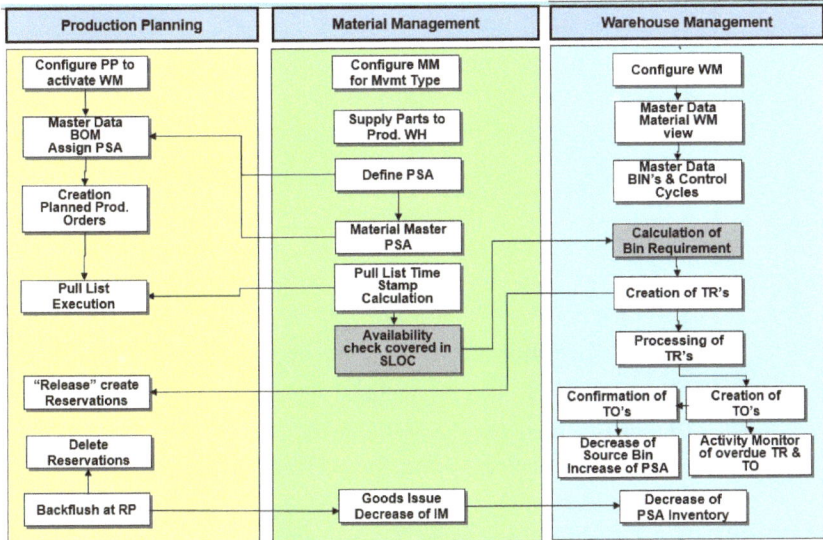

Production Planning	Material Management	Warehouse Management
Configure PP to activate WM	Configure MM for Mvmt Type	Configure WM
Master Data BOM Assign PSA	Supply Parts to Prod. WH	Master Data Material WM view
Creation Planned Prod. Orders	Define PSA	Master Data BIN's & Control Cycles
	Material Master PSA	Calculation of Bin Requirement
Pull List Execution	Pull List Time Stamp Calculation	Creation of TR's
	Availability check covered in SLOC	Processing of TR's
"Release" create Reservations		Confirmation of TO's / Creation of TO's
Delete Reservations		Decrease of Source Bin Increase of PSA / Activity Monitor of overdue TR & TO
Backflush at RP	Goods Issue Decrease of IM	Decrease of PSA Inventory

ment elements can be created for these missing parts. Components can be staged via direct stock transfer or using stock transfer reservations. Replenishment can also be triggered by setting a Kanban to 'empty' or creating transfer requirements in Warehouse Management.

The pull list is an integral part of the shop floor control, the replenishment for the production line uses planning, production order reservations and manual reservations to calculate the gross amount of materials per work center.

The replenishment takes into account the current stock situation on the work center, therefore it is vital that a time complaint backflush cycle is guaranteed to deliver a correct inventory snap-shot.

The net replenishment can be accessed by PSA (supply area/work center) and it also considers what replenishment quantities have already been initiated in an earlier run. In general, the replenishment of the production line with its work centers is a vital part to implement a successful SAP solution.

The pull-list:
- Is based on the detailed sequenced planned orders
- Is also a shortage information
- Flexible selection of component requirements
- Interface to WM for components
- Stock transfer (MM) or Transfer Order (WM) can be carried out

The pull-list function uses a supply to line calculation that consider:

- Are requirements covered by storage location stock, in other words is the material/component in the four walls of the plant, if no it is a missing part
- What quantity is actually available at the production supply area.
- This available stock is compared with the required quantities.
- WM staging for release order parts is carried out for the difference available and required quantity

Example:

1 = Total requirements
2 = Stock at the production storage bin level
3 = Reservations (equal to 4)
4 = Open Backflush Quantity from prior requested planned orders
5 = Available quantity in reserved storage
6 = Open Quantity based on existing TR/TO's (Feeder is supplying full cartons)
7 = The resulting quantity still to be staged (1 – 5 – 6)
8 = Quantity based on lot size (carton, etc.) our example is 20

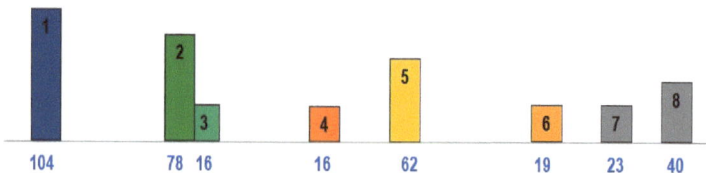

Warehouse Management

The intend of the warehouse activity monitor is, to assist and oversee, plan and optimize work processes in the warehouse. In case there are delays or errors in the overall system the activity monitor can used as an early warning system. The warehouse activity monitor helps you to identify and correct warehousing errors or critical processes soon after they occur, thus enabling you to carry out warehousing transactions in a timely manner.

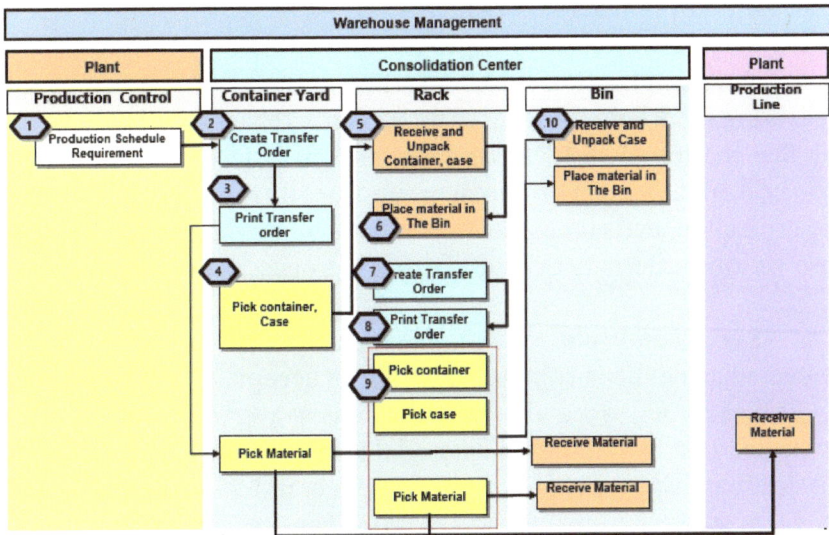

The warehouse activity monitor provides
- Automatic monitoring of warehousing processes
- Automatic recognition and display of errors in the warehouse
- Support in the analysis of processes in which errors have occurred
- Support for error correction

Why do I need the warehouse activity monitor? The warehouse monitor is useful for several reasons:

- Not all warehousing processes are carried out in the system without errors.
- Errors are often not recognized until sometime after they have occurred.
- The search for the cause of an error and correcting it can be time consuming.

Orders to move stock in the warehouse should always be processed within a reasonable time period. One of the key features of the warehouse monitoring task is the checking of timely processing of transfer orders in WM.

For example: If a brake pad has not been moved from the receiving dock into its destination within a few hours, then it could be that the transfer order has been lost, misplaced or that an error has occurred. Whether or not a process or situation is considered to be critical depends upon the object that is to be monitored. You can use various criteria to decide whether a process is critical:

As a general rule, you can say that a process is critical if the process has not been completed within an acceptable period of time. – For example, once the system creates a transfer order, it is expected that, as soon as the material has been physically moved to its destination in the warehouse, the transfer order will be confirmed.

When the system creates a posting change notice, soon afterwards, it is expected that the notice will be converted into transfer orders. For some activities in the warehouse, a deadline is set for the completion of the activity. This applies to – Supply of materials to production and – Delivery processing.

For some situations in WM, a certain period of time or duration is considered to be acceptable. These situations can be viewed as critical if the expected time span is exceeded. Examples include: Negative stock. As an example, negative stock is recorded in the goods receipt area if you post a goods receipts in WM before posting it in IM. Stock in interim storage types. For example, when you post a goods receipt in IM, the system stores this information in the interim storage area for goods receipts.

Warehouse Management Production Supply

The Warehouse Management (WM) application component is interfaced to the Planning Shop Floor Control (PP-SFC) application component to assist in providing materials to supply areas in the production line. Each Work-Center functioned as a supply area within the TRIM or CHASSY Line. The basic concept is to "supply" needed materials by creation of transfer requirements in WM. A Transfer Order (TO) is supplying needed materials to the storage bins (production supply) in the production line. The production completion creates a goods issue posting that reduces the stock quantity of materials that have been removed and used from the running production order at the specific work center.

For each material and production supply area in a plant, there are storage bins defined to which the necessary materials will be supplied and the type of material staging that will be implemented. This is known as a control cycle.

The system supports the following types of material staging:
- Pick Parts Production Order
- Crate Parts (not in use)
- Release Order Parts

You can request material staging in advance so that the required materials are supplied using WM (transfer requirement / transfer order). The WM system is set up for release order parts and if that fails (no control cycle record) the material will be handled as a pick part. Pick parts are materials that are provided in the required quantities as specified in a production order. These parts will be requested even if your actual stock level at the production supply bin is filled up.

Release order parts are requested independently of the orders. You can individual request the amount of materials to be supplied. This can be done directly on the work center screen for those parts that are either not controlled by the production supply process and are managed based on individual requests. The Warehouse Management System supports you by the following information:

- Requirement quantity according to the released orders
- Stock in the production storage bin and quantity to be placed into stock (transfer orders already requested but not confirmed)
- Open transfer requirements for the production storage bin

In addition, you can display information on the stock in quality inspection. On the basis of this information, you determine the required quantity manually. Release order parts are scheduled manually based on the requirements of production orders and the stock levels at the supply areas.

Using WM for material staging requires care and strict discipline in the system handling. If the needed stock is located in another location, it must be moved from that location to the production storage bin, because it is from that bin that the consumption posting (production completion goods issue 261) will take place. If this practice is not consequently followed, the efficient will be jeopardized by the increase in unnecessary stock on the production line.

Chapter 5: Manage Model Changes – Rapid and Lean

Inspiration for what is possible

Responding to the challenges of an ever-changing product value chain with SAP PLM

At its core, Product Lifecycle Management (PLM) provides an integrated approach to sharing and controlling critical data so products are built correctly, sourced properly, and priced accurately. It's a process that guides and manages a product offering from the first concept through end of the product's life. It's a broad discipline, spanning product development and supply chain issues. Truly cross-functional, it involves multiple core processes as well as the company's key design and supply partners.

In an increasingly competitive global marketplace, companies must be able to manage their portfolio of products and respond to changing demand with insight, speed, and accuracy. Product development, manufacturing, and distribution must evolve quickly to keep pace with customer needs and optimize overall cost. Success requires constant product innovation driven by customer needs, but that innovation needs to be managed. Companies must control how they apply innovation to various product segments while managing the common consequence of product proliferation.

As disruptive technologies drive innovation, harnessing it throughout the product lifecycle and creating a social feedback mechanism—not to mention getting buy-in from people who have clung to traditional processes—are crucial.

Another daunting challenge is regulatory compliance, especially for companies that operate globally and face several sets of regulations in various regions. Manufacturers face compliance requirements that call for strict controls over strategic sourcing (e.g., conflict minerals), product composition (e.g., RoHS, WEEE), manufacturing processes (e.g., GMP), and product performance (e.g., CAFE, FCC,

UL). These requirements significantly impact product complexity and call for meticulous management of product data. The risks of non-compliance are significant, including being shut out of lucrative markets.

PLM an in its core ECM (Engineering Change Management) exists to meet tough global business challenges. A SAP solution that advocate a business-led approach to PLM that aims first to uncover root causes—both organizational and industry-specific—and then implement solutions leveraging SAP's PLM suite.

PLM as competitive advantage

When planned and executed well, PLM implementations can significantly improve efficiency and effectiveness, both of which are vital as product development spreads across large ecosystems of partners, supply chains stretch around the globe, and regulatory pressures rise. SAP's PLM system is different than other enterprise systems such as CRM or SRM systems. The PLM system is integrated with manufacturing, sales, after market and other, and because the relevant business processes span so many groups, organizations, and systems, they can be very challenging to set up effectively. PLM is helping businesses manage product-related information across lifecycles, supply chains, and value chains in order to bolster revenue growth. To be successful, companies need to regard PLM as a critical business system, not simply a productivity tool.

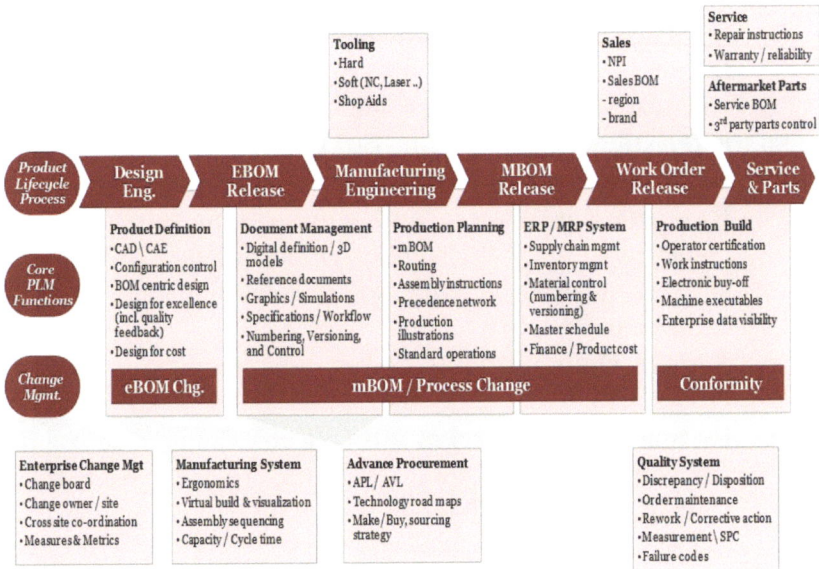

Service	
• Repair instructions	
• Warranty / reliability	

Tooling	Sales
• Hard	• NPI
• Soft (NC, Laser ..)	• Sales BOM
• Shop Aids	- region
	- brand

Aftermarket Parts
• Service BOM
• 3rd party parts control

Product Lifecycle Process: Design Eng. › EBOM Release › Manufacturing Engineering › MBOM Release › Work Order Release › Service & Parts

Core PLM Functions

Product Definition	Document Management	Production Planning	ERP / MRP System	Production Build
• CAD \ CAE	• Digital definition / 3D models	• mBOM	• Supply chain mgmt	• Operator certification
• Configuration control	• Reference documents	• Routing	• Inventory mgmt	• Work instructions
• BOM centric design	• Graphics / Simulations	• Assembly instructions	• Material control (numbering & versioning)	• Electronic buy-off
• Design for excellence (incl. quality feedback)	• Specifications / Workflow	• Precedence network	• Master schedule	• Machine executables
• Design for cost	• Numbering, Versioning, and Control	• Production illustrations	• Finance / Product cost	• Enterprise data visibility
		• Standard operations		

Change Mgmt: eBOM Chg. | mBOM / Process Change | Conformity

Enterprise Change Mgt	Manufacturing System	Advance Procurement	Quality System
• Change board	• Ergonomics	• APL / AVL	• Discrepancy / Disposition
• Change owner / site	• Virtual build & visualization	• Technology road maps	• Order maintenance
• Cross site co-ordination	• Assembly sequencing	• Make / Buy, sourcing strategy	• Rework / Corrective action
• Measures & Metrics	• Capacity / Cycle time		• Measurement \ SPC
			• Failure codes

Example: Manage Model Changes – Manage Configuration

Impact on your business

Product development, manufacturing, and distribution are business functions that are built for a robust PLM system to deliver true value by providing the following benefits:

- A **single source of truth** for product information serves as the common collaboration platform, enabling both internal and external collaboration and speeding up product design, prototyping, and production.
- **Uniform & Best Business processes** are supported by leading practice, process optimization and workflow automation to bring consistency while reducing process cycle times.
- **Identification of quality issues** and linking them to the product bill of material (BoM) helps close the loop from detection to correction, providing an efficient framework for continuous product quality improvement.
- **Improved product and portfolio management** capabilities for managing product variants cater to market-specific demands.
- **Accurate tracking of raw material and component characteristics** and costs in BoM drive improved vendor management and reduction in overall product cost.
- **Raw material source and composition information** is managed in the PLM solution in accordance with compliance standards, helping to reduce the risk of non-compliance.
- **Supply chain optimization** speeds production and improves efficiency.
- **Reduced time to market** helps cut costs and increase agility and competitiveness.
- **Complete control of production data** makes regional compliance easier.

Example: Automotive Vehicle Live-Cycle

A vehicle spans the entire lifecycle and creates and manages data that differentiates the automotive industry performance on a market and operating basis. Integrated change management enables consistent, timely incorporation on global basis. The ability to collaborate using the same environment and data structure speeds time to value.

Overall a good master data base that is maintained by Engineering Change Management (ECM) represents an infrastructure investment that enables the automotive industry, to establish a *Global Platforms:* modular design, design reuse, standardization, *Global Procurement:* common nomenclature, common parts, value analysis, *Global Build:* standard (visual) work, flexible manufacturing, integrated quality and a *Global Service:* linked tech pubs, common service bills, global parts database

The PLM process is defined by a series of detailed specifications that cover end-to-end product workflow and change management across functions (design, plan, build, service). Specifications are grouped into functionality sets and are aligned to the PLM capability framework.

- *CAD to mBOM*: product definition, parts list, drawings, configuration & BOM management
- *mBOM use and external data:* create process plans, releasing mBOM and external systems

- ***Production orders and quality:*** manage shop floor build instructions, non-conformance and BOM reconciliation
- ***Change & Document Management:*** control of product configuration change across design and manufacturing sites. Document control through product lifecycle process.

Chapter 6: Potential Timeline / Schedule

It is very difficult to estimate how long it will take for an automtive company, that depends on scope, resources and team size. However, referring to the SAP solution that went live and is described in this book it took thirty month to go live.

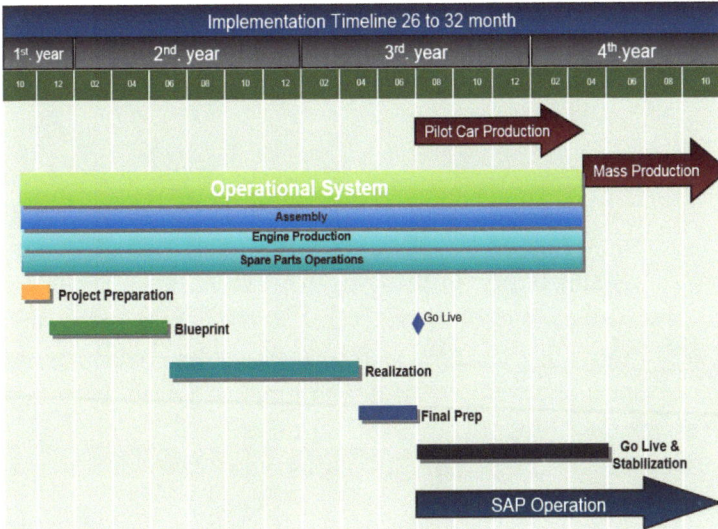

Chapter 7: Considering HANA

The musles of a real-time automotive solutions with HANA® will become the differentiator through vehicle innovation, to reduce operational costs, react quickly to change independent of the high complexity, and increasing productivity. Automotive companies must innovate quicker, increase efficiency, and manufacture more vehicles based on specific customer requirements. The vehicle of the future will be customer specific and no longer model based with a specific set of options.

To satisfy this changing world of changing requirements, an automotive company need speed to transform into a customer driven business. It is critical that an automotive company can identify new desirable products and is fast in bringing it to market while giving the end customer full control of the selection of the vehicle specifics. One of the first innovative changes will be a customer specific paint job, no longer that a specific model is available in white, blue, red etc. Racing strips, paint layouts, picture based etc. will become part of the customer experience. This all will be possible due to the revolution that HANA® will bring.

Support new business processes that use HANA in the automotive industry and drive improved, more flexible manufacturing and logistics processes while reacting to changes and disruptions without any interuptions. Achieve immediate results of complex re-sequencing and inventory management data.

Cut costs with real-time updates on demand changes and supply chain situations, and make new planning and MRP possible in minutes, to

Production Planning and Execution

Operational Procurement and Inbound Logistics for Direct Material

Lean Manufacturing

Sequenced Manufacturing

Outbound Logistics

Demand and Supply Planning

ensure that production and purchasing is aligned with the new situation.

Optimize production and supply chain by switching over to collaborative network planning. In the past, this was very diffucult to achieve due to the enormous amount of data required to recMESulate, today HANA as a gamechanger will create significant new opportunities for automotive companies. HANA will allow companies to rapidly process and adjust to situation as well as allow to have the time to initiate simulations (what-ifs) for more profit optimization and manufacturing efficiency.

bookforces
Publishing - Miami USA

Recognized as one of the foremost, innovative publishing company, bookforces specializes in publishing books that are on the leading edge. To be succesful we go all-out to be ahead of the curve.

Bookforces titles comprise a wide range of categories and interests, including important business specific works like this one. Our view point is that business is really global in every way, and that today's readers are looking for to be inspired and educated. To discovery more about what we're publishing, please check out:

www.bookforces.com

www.ingramcontent.com/pod-product-compliance
Lightning Source LLC
Chambersburg PA
CBHW041228270326
41935CB00002B/9